Quick and Easy
Stir-fry
Cookbook

Quick and Easy Stir-fry Cookbook

by

Carol Palmer

foulsham
LONDON • NEW YORK • TORONTO • SYDNEY

foulsham

The Publishing House, Bennetts Close,
Cippenham, Slough, Berkshire SL1 5AP, England

Dedication:
To my dear husband Phil and my children Emma and Joe

ISBN 0-572-02382-0

Typeset in Great Britain by Grafica, Bournemouth.
Printed in Great Britain by Cox & Wyman Ltd, Reading

CONTENTS

★

INTRODUCTION

★

My experience of stir-frying dates back to my years as a Home Economics student living away from home for the first time with a fellow student in very basic digs. She bought me a wok for my twenty-first birthday and this was to be one of our few pieces of cooking equipment. Grants being small, we would scour the supermarkets and markets of East Croydon for bargains to feed our healthy appetites. As a consequence, practically all our meals were stir-fried! We didn't just survive, we thrived! Both cooking and eating were enjoyable; we never tired of our experiments but were spurred on to develop further ideas which we practised on each other, friends and family. Fourteen years on, we still visit each others' homes and don't feel inhibited by producing our woks from the cupboard to stir-fry the evening meal. Perhaps it was this early experience in my cooking life that showed me the versatility of stir-frying as a method of cooking. Yet to most people 'stir-frying' still conjures up a picture of the cook vigorously stirring an array of Chinese vegetables in a wok. Wrong! Unfortunately, stir-frying has taken on an image that doesn't do it justice. It is simply a method of cooking that involves the frequent, not constant, stirring of ingredients in a small amount of very hot oil in either a wok or a large heavy-based frying pan.

Stir-frying may have originated in China as a means of cooking food quickly and efficiently when fuel was scarce, but stir-fry dishes do not have to be Chinese in their origin or make-up. This book aims to show the enthusiastic and adventurous cook how to stir-fry a vast range of savoury and sweet dishes with a world-wide theme that may not necessarily be associated with stir-frying. The ingredients used are readily available and generally modestly priced. Like all stir-fry recipes, these are simple to follow and quick to prepare. However, you will find that they lend themselves equally well to both the family dinner table and the supper party menu.

STIR-FRY TECHNIQUES

★

There are few rules for stir-frying, but to get the best results from these recipes the following guidelines should help.

1. The Utensils: A wok or large heavy-based frying pan (skillet) can be used and in some cases a large heavy-based saucepan. Woks are ideal as their depth means more food can be accommodated than in a frying pan and there is less risk of it being spilt when tossed in the oil. Also, their shape means less oil is required and the heat is rapidly distributed over the surface which aids the cooking process. Woks are traditionally round-based although flat-based ones suitable for use on electric cookers are now available. The round-based woks are really safe to use only on a gas hob. If you have decided to buy a wok, choose a deep-sided one as large as you can accommodate and as heavy as possible, preferably made from carbon steel.

For stirring, metal stir-fry spatulas are available. However, there is no need to go out and buy one of these; a long-handled metal fish slice or spatula or even a metal spoon will do the job just as well.

2. The Method: The key to effective stir-frying is to have all the ingredients prepared first so that you can concentrate on the cooking process and have no need to leave the pan. The second important step is to ensure that the wok or pan is heated until very hot before adding the oil. Next, add the oil and gently swirl around the pan to ensure that all areas are coated with hot oil, thus preventing sticking and making sure all pieces of food are subjected to the same temperature. The pan should be nearly smoking before you add the food; test the temperature with one piece of food first before adding the full quantity. If cooking garlic, ginger or chillis first, it is best if the oil is not quite this hot or they will burn and turn bitter. When you are confident that the oil is the correct temperature, proceed with the recipe, adding the ingredients to the pan as directed and gently tossing them in the hot oil. Remember, it is not essential to stir constantly, in fact for some ingredients such as meat it is important to allow it to spend time in contact with the pan surface so that it browns and cooks before stirring further. Move the food from the centre of the pan to the sides to ensure even cooking. Stir-fried food should not be greasy if it has been cooked correctly in the right amount of oil and it should have slightly more bite than food cooked byconventional methods.

3. The Food: Generally, most foods can be stir-fried, but the amount of time required will vary with the texture and density of the individual food. It is essential that ingredients are cut into fine small pieces or strips of about the same size so that the hot oil penetrates and quickly cooks the food. Large pieces would take too long to cook and could end up greasy and unappetising. It is best to use the leaner, more tender cuts of meat as stir-frying is too rapid a method of cooking to tenderise tougher meat adequately. Always ensure that meat is cut across the grain to prevent toughness. Each recipe describes how the ingredients should be cut but generally where it says the meat should be cut into fine strips, these should be no thicker than 5 mm/¼ in and 5–7.5 cm/2–3 in long. Fish pieces should be slightly thicker as, like some fruits and cake, it has a delicate texture and requires a certain degree of care in stir-frying. Gentle stirring and a short cooking time should prevent the food from disintegrating. In some cases it may be necessary to blanch or par-boil ingredients before stir-frying to soften them slightly, but details for this or other specific preparation techniques are given in the individual recipes.

4. The Oil: It is important to use oil that does not break down at high temperatures. Groundnut (peanut) oil is ideal as it has a mild, pleasant flavour; however, this can prove rather expensive if you are planning to do a lot of stir-frying and is rather high in saturated fats. Corn oil, sunflower oil and most blended vegetable oils are cheaper and suitable for stir-frying and a healthier option as their saturated fat content is much lower.

Once the basic preparation for stir-frying has been carried out, you can proceed to conjure up untold delights from your wok or frying pan. The recipes in this book illustrate just how easy it is to stir-fry the most impressive dishes and will leave you wanting to experiment further with this quick and easy method of cooking.

NOTES ON THE RECIPES

- All cooking times given in this book are approximate and depend upon the heat source, size of pieces of food, and the cooking utensil used. Adjust the cooking time accordingly to ensure the food is adequately cooked but remember the vegetables should retain some bite.

- The amount of oil required for stir-frying may need to be increased slightly if you are using a frying pan (skillet) rather than a wok.

- If it appears that the contents of the pan are drying out or 'catching', do not add more oil at this stage as it will make the food greasy but add a little water instead.

- Follow either metric, Imperial or American measures, and never be tempted to interchange.

- All spoon measurements are level.

- Eggs are large.

SPEEDY STARTERS

★

Pears with Melting Stilton

SERVES 4	METRIC	IMPERIAL	AMERICAN
Groundnut (peanut) oil	10 ml	2 tsp	2 tsp
Small red onion, finely chopped	1	1	1
Firm, ripe pears, peeled, cored and cubed	4	4	4
Balsamic or red wine vinegar	15 ml	1 tbsp	1 tbsp
Stilton, diced	100 g	4 oz	1 cup
Salt and freshly ground black pepper			
A few endive or curly lettuce leaves			

✳

1 Heat the wok or a large, deep frying pan.

2 Pour the oil into the pan and when hot add the onion and stir-fry for about 1 minute or until the onion is transparent.

3 Add the pear and stir-fry for a further minute.

4 Stir in the vinegar, then throw in the Stilton and turn briskly and briefly in the pan.

5 Season to taste. Serve the pears with the melting Stilton on lettuce leaves on individual plates.

PREPARATION TIME: 5 MINUTES COOKING TIME: 5 MINUTES

Summer Crab Starter

SERVES 4	METRIC	IMPERIAL	AMERICAN
Oil	*15 ml*	*1 tbsp*	*1 tbsp*
Shallot, finely chopped	*1*	*1*	*1*
Small leek, thinly sliced	*1*	*1*	*1*
White crabmeat	*225 g*	*8 oz*	*1 cup*
Lemon, juice and zest only	*½*	*½*	*½*
Crème fraîche	*150 ml*	*¼ pt*	*⅔ cup*
Salt and freshly ground black pepper			
For the topping:			
Oil	*15 ml*	*1 tbsp*	*1 tbsp*
Sliced white bread, crusts removed and cut into 1 cm/½ in cubes	*2*	*2*	*2*
Chopped fresh dill (dill weed)	*10 ml*	*2 tsp*	*2 tsp*

1   Heat the wok or a large heavy-based frying pan.

2   Pour in the oil and when hot throw in the shallot and leek and stir-fry for 1–2 minutes until both are softened.

3   Gently stir in the crabmeat, lemon juice and zest and crème fraîche. Season to taste and heat through. Transfer the mixture to 4 ramekins (custard cups) and keep warm.

4   To make the topping, wipe out the wok or frying pan with kitchen paper and return it to the heat.

5   Add the oil to the pan and when very hot, drop in the bread cubes and stir-fry for about 2 minutes or until tinged brown.

6   Mix the dill with the bread cubes and then sprinkle over the crab mixture in the ramekins.

PREPARATION TIME:
5 MINUTES

COOKING TIME:
8 MINUTES

Sweet Shallots

SERVES 4	METRIC	IMPERIAL	AMERICAN
Oil	30 ml	2 tbsp	2 tbsp
Small shallots, peeled and halved	350 g	12 oz	3 cups
Sprig of fresh thyme	1	1	1
Sprig of fresh rosemary	1	1	1
Salt	2.5 ml	½ tsp	½ tsp
Black pepper			
Maple syrup	30 ml	2 tbsp	2 tbsp
Vegetable stock	150 ml	¼ pt	⅔ cup
Honey-roast ham, diced	100 g	4 oz	1 cup

❋

1   Heat the wok or a large heavy-based frying pan.

2   Pour the oil into the pan and when hot add all the shallots and stir-fry for 3–6 minutes until they start to soften and turn translucent.

3   Add all the remaining ingredients except the ham to the pan. Stir well. Cover the pan, reduce the heat slightly and simmer for 10 minutes.

4   Remove the lid from the pan and stir in the ham.

5   Turn the heat up full and boil for about a minute to reduce the amount of liquid slightly.

6   Serve hot.

PREPARATION TIME:
5 MINUTES

COOKING TIME:
18 MINUTES

Stir-fry Soup

SERVES 4	METRIC	IMPERIAL	AMERICAN
Oil	15 ml	1 tbsp	1 tbsp
Garlic clove, crushed	1	1	1
Very finely chopped fresh root ginger	5 ml	1 tsp	1 tsp
Spring onions (scallions), very finely chopped	6	6	6
Red (bell) pepper finely diced	½	½	½
Baby sweetcorn (corn), fresh or thawed frozen, finely sliced	4	4	4
Mangetout (snow peas), finely sliced	25 g	1 oz	1 oz
Dry sherry	30 ml	2 tbsp	2 tbsp
Soy sauce	25 ml	1½ tbsp	1½ tbsp
Brown sugar	10 ml	2 tsp	2 tsp
Pinch of five-spice powder			
Chicken or good vegetable stock	900 ml	1½ pts	3¾ cups

1 Heat the wok or a large saucepan.

2 Add the oil and when hot stir-fry the garlic, ginger and spring onions for about 1 minute.

3 Add the red pepper, sweetcorn and mangetout to the pan and cook for a further 1–2 minutes until the sweetcorn slices are slightly softened.

4 Mix in the remaining ingredients and bring the soup just to the boil, stirring occasionally.

5 Reduce the heat and simmer for 5 minutes.

SERVING SUGGESTION

Serve hot, ensuring that everybody has some of each of the vegetables in their soup.

PREPARATION TIME: COOKING TIME:
10 MINUTES   10 MINUTES

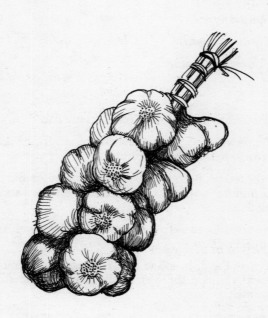

❋
The Italian Job

SERVES 4	METRIC	IMPERIAL	AMERICAN
Oil	15 ml	1 tbsp	1 tbsp
Garlic clove, crushed	1	1	1
Onion, sliced	1	1	1
Small red (bell) pepper, diced	½	½	½
Mushrooms, sliced	100 g	4 oz	4 oz
Ripe tomatoes, skinned and quartered	4	4	4
Chopped fresh oregano	15 ml	1 tbsp	1 tbsp
Tomato purée (paste)	15 ml	1 tbsp	1 tbsp
Black olives, pitted (stoned)	12	12	12
Mozzarella cheese, drained and diced	100 g	4 oz	1 cup

❋

1 Heat the wok or a large heavy-based frying pan.

2 Pour the oil into the pan and when hot stir in the garlic and onion and cook for about 1 minute.

3 Stir in the red pepper, mushrooms and tomatoes and cook for about 2 minutes until the tomatoes have softened and started to break down.

4 Add the oregano, tomato purée and olives, stir well and cook for a further minute.

5 To complete the dish, spoon the very hot mixture into warm bowls and sprinkle the Mozzarella over the top so that it starts to melt.

PREPARATION TIME: COOKING TIME:
15 MINUTES   6 MINUTES

Piquant Chicken

SERVES 4	METRIC	IMPERIAL	AMERICAN
Oil	15 ml	1 tbsp	1 tbsp
Garlic clove, crushed	1	1	1
Small onion, finely chopped	1	1	1
Chicken breast, cut into thin strips	225 g	8 oz	8 oz
Tinned peach halves, very finely chopped	4	4	4
Medium-hot curry paste	15 ml	1 tbsp	1 tbsp
Tomato purée (paste)	15 ml	1 tbsp	1 tbsp
Salt and freshly ground black pepper			
Sweet white wine	45 ml	3 tbsp	3 tbsp
Lemon juice	10 ml	2 tsp	2 tsp
Double (heavy) cream	150 ml	¼ pt	⅔ cup

1   Heat the wok or a large heavy-based frying pan.

2   Heat the oil, then add the garlic and onion and stir-fry for about 1 minute.

3   Add the chicken to the pan and stir-fry for 1–2 minutes or until it has changed colour.

4   Add the peaches, curry paste, tomato purée and salt and pepper and stir well.

5   Gradually blend the wine and lemon juice into the mixture in the pan.

6   Bring to the boil and cook for several minutes to reduce.

7   Stir in the cream and heat through without boiling.

PREPARATION TIME: COOKING TIME:
5 MINUTES   8 MINUTES

Stir-fried Scallops with Smoked Bacon

SERVES 4	METRIC	IMPERIAL	AMERICAN
Scallops, fresh or thawed frozen	12	12	12
Oil	15 ml	1 tbsp	1 tbsp
Small red onion, finely chopped	1	1	1
Thick smoked bacon, finely cubed	100 g	4 oz	4 oz
Lemon juice	5 ml	1 tsp	1 tsp
Few drops of Worcestershire sauce			
Pinch of salt			
Pinch of sugar			
Chopped fresh parsley	15 ml	1 tbsp	1 tbsp

1 If using fresh scallops, detach them from their shells, wash them and then pat them dry.

2 Cut each scallop into about 4 slices.

3 Heat the wok or a large heavy-based frying pan, then pour in the oil and heat it.

4 Stir-fry the onion for about 1 minute.

5 Add the bacon to the pan and cook for a further minute.

6 Add the scallops and stir-fry until their edges are starting to curl.

7 Finally, stir in the remaining ingredients and serve.

PREPARATION TIME: 10 MINUTES COOKING TIME: 7 MINUTES

Creamy Mixed Mushrooms

SERVES 4	METRIC	IMPERIAL	AMERICAN
Oil	30 ml	2 tbsp	2 tbsp
Garlic clove, crushed	1	1	1
Shallot, finely chopped	1	1	1
Chestnut mushrooms, quartered	100 g	4 oz	4 oz
Flat dark-gilled mushrooms, thickly sliced	100 g	4 oz	4 oz
Shiitake mushrooms, halved	100 g	4 oz	4 oz
Oyster mushrooms, halved	100 g	4 oz	4 oz
White wine	45 ml	3 tbsp	3 tbsp
Double (heavy) cream	150 ml	¼ pt	⅔ cup
Salt and freshly ground black pepper			

1 Heat the wok or a large heavy-based frying pan.

2 Pour in the oil and when hot stir in the garlic and shallot and cook for about 1 minute.

3 Add the chestnut mushrooms to the pan and stir-fry for a further minute.

4 Add the remaining mushrooms and stir-fry for about 2 minutes or until they are starting to soften.

5 Pour the wine into the pan and cook, stirring, until the amount of wine is slightly reduced.

6 Add the cream and seasoning, stir gently and heat through.

7 Serve hot.

PREPARATION TIME:
10 MINUTES

COOKING TIME:
10 MINUTES

Aubergine and Anchovy Appetiser

SERVES 4	METRIC	IMPERIAL	AMERICAN
Aubergines (eggplants)	450 g	1 lb	1 lb
Salt			
Oil	15 ml	1 tbsp	1 tbsp
Small onion, finely chopped	1	1	1
Garlic cloves, crushed	2	2	2
Ripe tomatoes, skinned and quartered	3	3	3
Tomato purée (paste)	10 ml	2 tsp	2 tsp
Tinned anchovies, drained	50 g	2 oz	2 oz
Pinch of sugar			
Freshly ground black pepper			

1 Cut the aubergines into 2.5cm/1 in cubes, sprinkle with salt and leave for about 20 minutes.

2 Rinse the aubergines in cold water, drain, then pat dry.

3 Heat the wok or a deep heavy-based frying pan. Add the oil and heat.

4 Stir fry the onion and garlic until the onion is transparent.

5 Add the tomatoes and stir-fry for about 30 seconds until soft.

6 Stir in the remaining ingredients, adding a little water if the mixture seems too dry.

7 Cover the pan, reduce the heat and braise for about 3 minutes.

8 Stir, then serve hot in small individual bowls.

PREPARATION TIME: **COOKING TIME:**
30 MINUTES   7 MINUTES

Avocados at Sea

SERVES 4	METRIC	IMPERIAL	AMERICAN
Avocado pears, ripe but firm	2	2	2
Oil	15 ml	1 tbsp	1 tbsp
Garlic clove, crushed	1	1	1
Mixed shellfish, e.g. mussels, prawns (shrimp), cockles, squid, fresh or thawed frozen	450 g	1 lb	1 lb
Salt and freshly ground black pepper			
Lemon juice	15 ml	1 tbsp	1 tbsp

1 Peel the avocados, remove the stones (pits) and cut the flesh into 2.5 cm/1 in cubes.

2 Heat the wok or a large heavy-based frying pan.

3 Add the oil and when it is hot add the garlic and stir-fry quickly and briefly.

4 Place the shellfish in the pan and stir-fry for 1–2 minutes.

5 Stir in the seasoning and lemon juice.

6 Mix in the avocado cubes, being careful not to break them up.

7 Serve hot.

PREPARATION TIME: COOKING TIME:
5 MINUTES   5 MINUTES

Green Peppered Onions

SERVES 4	METRIC	IMPERIAL	AMERICAN
Oil	15 ml	1 tbsp	1 tbsp
Large onions, sliced	2	2	2
Large red onions, sliced	2	2	2
Brown sugar	15 ml	1 tbsp	1 tbsp
Green peppercorns, roughly crushed	15 ml	1 tbsp	1 tbsp
Pinch of salt			
Thin French bread slices, lightly toasted	4	4	4

※

1 Heat the wok or a large heavy-based frying pan.

2 Pour the oil into the pan and heat, then add the onions and stir-fry for 1–2 minutes until softened.

3 Stir in the sugar, peppercorns and salt.

4 Spoon the onion mixture on to slices of French bread and serve hot.

PREPARATION TIME: 10 MINUTES   COOKING TIME: 5 MINUTES

Sesame Melbas with Prawns

SERVES 4	METRIC	IMPERIAL	AMERICAN
Thick white bread slices	3	3	3
Egg, beaten	1	1	1
Sesame seeds	30 ml	2 tbsp	2 tbsp
Oil	45 ml	3 tbsp	3 tbsp
Cooked prawns (shrimp)	225 g	8 oz	2 cups
Lemon juice	30 ml	2 tbsp	2 tbsp

1 Remove and discard the crusts from the bread, then cut into 2.5 cm/1 in cubes.

2 Dip the cubes in the egg and then into the sesame seeds.

3 Heat the wok or a large heavy-based frying pan.

4 Pour in the oil and when it is hot add the bread cubes, a few at a time, and stir-fry until they are lightly browned all over.

5 Stir in the prawns carefully. Heat through for 30–60 seconds.

6 Serve in individual bowls with the lemon juice drizzled over the top.

PREPARATION TIME: COOKING TIME:
5 MINUTES 5 MINUTES

Saucy Beans

SERVES 4	METRIC	IMPERIAL	AMERICAN
Oil	15 ml	1 tbsp	1 tbsp
Garlic clove, crushed	1	1	1
Finely chopped fresh root ginger	5 ml	1 tsp	1 tsp
Leek, finely sliced	1	1	1
Small red (bell) pepper, diced	½	½	½
Can kidney beans, drained	430 g	15 oz	1 large
Can borlotti beans, drained	430 g	15 oz	1 large
Black bean sauce	15 ml	1 tbsp	1 tbsp

✳

1 Heat the wok or a large heavy-based frying pan.

2 Pour in the oil and when hot add the garlic and ginger and stir-fry for about 30 seconds.

3 Add the leek and red pepper to the pan and cook for 1–2 minutes until they lose their crispness.

4 Stir in all the beans and the black bean sauce.

5 Heat through and serve in individual bowls.

PREPARATION TIME: COOKING TIME:
5 MINUTES   5 MINUTES

Mussels with Mushrooms and Garlic

SERVES 4	METRIC	IMPERIAL	AMERICAN
Oil	15 ml	1 tbsp	1 tbsp
Garlic cloves, crushed	2	2	2
Button mushrooms, quartered	225 g	8 oz	8 oz
Shelled mussels, fresh or thawed frozen	225 g	8 oz	8 oz
Chopped fresh parsley	15 ml	1 tbsp	1 tbsp
Chopped fresh chives	15 ml	1 tbsp	1 tbsp
Ground black pepper			

1 Heat the wok or a large heavy-based frying pan.

2 Add the oil and heat, then add the garlic and stir-fry for a few seconds.

3 Add the mushrooms and cook for about 1 minute

4 Add the mussels, parsley and chives and a little black pepper and cook for a further minute or so.

SERVING SUGGESTION

Serve hot with fresh crusty bread.

**PREPARATION TIME:
5 MINUTES**

**COOKING TIME:
4 MINUTES**

FISHY
FEASTS

★

Seafood Fried Rice

SERVES 4	METRIC	IMPERIAL	AMERICAN
Oil	30 ml	2 tbsp	2 tbsp
Garlic cloves, crushed	2	2	2
Onion, finely chopped	1	1	1
Leek, finely sliced	1	1	1
Mild green chilli, very finely chopped	1	1	1
Small red (bell) pepper, diced	1	1	1
Smoked bacon, finely chopped	25 g	1 oz	1 oz
Mixed shellfish, e.g. mussels prawns (shrimp), squid fresh or thawed frozen	350 g	12 oz	12 oz
Cold cooked long-grain rice	450 g	1 lb	4 cups
Salt	2.5 ml	½ tsp	½ tsp
Chopped fresh parsley	30 ml	2 tbsp	2 tbsp

1 Heat the wok or a large heavy-based frying pan and pour in the oil.

2 When the oil is hot, stir-fry the garlic, onion, leek and chilli for 1–2 minutes or until the leek and onion have started to soften.

3 Add the pepper and bacon and cook for a further minute.

4 Add the shellfish, rice and salt and stir thoroughly, ensuring that the mixture is hot all the way through.

5 Serve hot with the parsley sprinkled over.

PREPARATION TIME: COOKING TIME:
15 MINUTES   7 MINUTES

Special Stir-fried Huss

SERVES 4	METRIC	IMPERIAL	AMERICAN
Oil	15 ml	1 tbsp	1 tbsp
Garlic clove, crushed	1	1	1
Shallot, finely chopped	1	1	1
Smoked bacon, finely diced	100 g	4 oz	4 oz
Mangetout (snow peas) trimmed	75 g	3 oz	3 oz
Baby sweetcorn (corn), fresh or thawed frozen	75 g	3 oz	3 oz
Mushrooms, quartered	50 g	2 oz	2 oz
Huss, skinned, boned and cut into 2.5 cm/1 in cubes	225 g	8 oz	8 oz
Dry sherry	5 ml	1 tsp	1 tsp
Soy sauce	5 ml	1 tsp	1 tsp
Yellow bean sauce	10 ml	2 tsp	2 tsp
Pinch of sugar			

1   Heat the wok or a large heavy-based frying pan.

2   Pour in the oil and when very hot add the garlic and shallot and stir-fry for about 30 seconds.

3   Add the bacon, mangetout, sweetcorn and mushrooms to the pan and cook for a further 2 minutes.

4   Gently stir in the fish and cook for about 1 minute.

5 Add the remaining ingredients and cook for 1–2 minutes, stirring carefully to avoid breaking the fish.

SERVING SUGGESTION

Serve hot with boiled rice.

<table>
<tr><td>PREPARATION TIME:
15 MINUTES</td><td></td><td>COOKING TIME:
8 MINUTES</td></tr>
</table>

Whiting with Pesto Sauce

SERVES 4	METRIC	IMPERIAL	AMERICAN
Pine kernels	30 ml	2 tbsp	2 tbsp
Oil	15 ml	1 tbsp	1 tbsp
Whiting fillets, cut into thick strips	450 g	1 lb	1 lb
Tub fresh pesto sauce	120 g	4½ oz	4½ oz

1 Toast the pine kernels under the grill (broiler) until lightly browned.

2 Heat the wok or a large heavy-based frying pan.

3 Add the oil and when hot stir-fry the fish for about 2 minutes, being careful not to break it up.

4 Pour in the pesto sauce, stir and cook for a further minute or so to heat the sauce thoroughly.

5 Serve hot, sprinkled with the pine kernels.

PREPARATION TIME: 5 MINUTES COOKING TIME: 5 MINUTES

Blue Cheese Fish

SERVES 4	METRIC	IMPERIAL	AMERICAN
Oil	15 ml	1 tbsp	1 tbsp
Shallot, finely chopped	1	1	1
Celery, finely sliced	50 g	2 oz	2 oz
Mushrooms, sliced	100 g	4 oz	4 oz
Firm white fish fillet, e.g. cod, pollack, haddock, cut into thick strips	450 g	1 lb	1 lb
Double (heavy) cream	45 ml	3 tbsp	3 tbsp
Soured (dairy sour) cream	45 ml	3 tbsp	3 tbsp
Blue cheese, crumbled	75 g	3 oz	¾ cup
Salt and freshly ground black pepper			

1 Heat the wok or a large heavy-based frying pan.

2 Pour in the oil and when hot add the shallot and celery and cook for about 1 minute.

3 Add the mushrooms and fish to the pan and stir-fry carefully for a further minute.

4 Pour in the creams and sprinkle in the cheese and cook, stirring, for 1–2 minutes so that the fish cooks and the cheese melts.

5 Season to taste and serve.

PREPARATION TIME: COOKING TIME:
10 MINUTES   5 MINUTES

Thai-style Fish with Prawns

SERVES 4	METRIC	IMPERIAL	AMERICAN
Oil	15 ml	1 tbsp	1 tbsp
Garlic cloves, crushed	3	3	3
Chopped fresh root ginger	10 ml	2 tbsp	2 tbsp
Chopped fresh lemon grass	15 ml	1 tbsp	1 tbsp
Shallots, finely chopped	2	2	2
Chilli powder	5 ml	1 tsp	1 tsp
Firm white fish fillet, cut into thick strips	450 g	1 lb	1 lb
Tinned coconut milk	300 ml	½ pt	1¼ cups
Salt	2.5 ml	½ tsp	½ tsp
Thai fish sauce	10 ml	2 tsp	2 tsp
Lime juice	10 ml	2 tsp	2 tsp
Cooked prawns (shrimp)	100 g	4 oz	1 cup
Chopped fresh coriander (cilantro)	10 ml	2 tsp	2 tsp

1 Heat the wok or a large heavy-based frying pan. Add the oil and heat.
2 Add the garlic, ginger, lemon grass and shallots and stir-fry for about 1 minute.
3 Stir in the chilli powder, then carefully add the fish and stir-fry for about 1 minute.
4 Gently stir in the coconut milk, salt, fish sauce and lime juice and cook, stirring, for a further 1–2 minutes.
5 Finally, stir in the prawns and serve garnished with the chopped coriander.

SERVING SUGGESTION

Serve with rice.

PREPARATION TIME:
15 MINUTES

COOKING TIME:
7 MINUTES

Chilli Stir-fried Squid

SERVES 4	METRIC	IMPERIAL	AMERICAN
Oil	30 ml	2 tbsp	2 tbsp
Garlic cloves, crushed	2	2	2
Chopped fresh root ginger	10 ml	2 tsp	2 tsp
Small fresh red chilli, finely chopped	1	1	1
Fresh mild green chilli, very finely chopped	1	1	1
Spring onions (scallions)	5	5	5
Yellow (bell) pepper, diced	½	½	½
Cornflour (cornstarch)	5 ml	1 tsp	1 tsp
Water	60 ml	4 tbsp	4 tbsp
Dry sherry	30 ml	2 tbsp	2 tbsp
Soy sauce	30 ml	2 tbsp	2 tbsp
Oyster sauce	10 ml	2 tsp	2 tsp
Squid, cut into rings fresh or thawed frozen	450 g	1 lb	1 lb

1 Heat the wok or a large heavy-based frying pan.

2 Pour in the oil and when very hot add the garlic, ginger and chillis and cook for about 2 minutes.

3 Add the spring onions and pepper and stir-fry for 1 minute.

4 Blend the cornflour with the water and add this to the pan with the sherry, sauces and the squid.

5 Cook for about 1 minute, stirring constantly, or until the sauce has thickened and the squid has turned white.

SERVING SUGGESTION

Serve with rice or pasta.

PREPARATION TIME:
10 MINUTES

COOKING TIME:
7 MINUTES

Fish in a Green Coat

SERVES 4	METRIC	IMPERIAL	AMERICAN
Oil	30 ml	2 tbsp	2 tbsp
Firm white fish fillet, e.g. cod, haddock, whiting, cut into thick strips	450 g	1 lb	1 lb
Garlic clove, crushed	1	1	1
Leeks, finely sliced	2	2	2
Chopped fresh dill (dill weed)	15 ml	1 tbsp	1 tbsp
Chopped fresh parsley	30 ml	2 tbsp	2 tbsp
Fresh spinach, finely shredded	100 g	4 oz	4 oz
Pinch of grated nutmeg			
White wine	60 ml	4 tbsp	4 tbsp
Crème fraîche	30 ml	2 tbsp	2 tbsp
Salt and freshly ground black pepper			

1   Heat the wok or a large heavy-based frying pan.

2   Pour in the oil and when very hot add the fish and stir-fry gently for about 1–2 minutes, being careful not to break it up.

3   Lift the fish out of the pan with a draining spoon and transfer to a plate. Keep warm.

4   Reheat the pan and add the garlic, leeks, chopped herbs, spinach and nutmeg. Stir-fry for about 2–3 minutes or until the leeks are quite soft.

5   Add the wine to the pan and bring it to the boil, stirring, and cook for several minutes to reduce the amount of wine slightly.

6   Stir in the crème fraîche and then return the fish to the pan.

7   Season to taste and heat through.

SERVING SUGGESTION

Serve with creamed potatoes and a selection of hot vegetables.

PREPARATION TIME: COOKING TIME:
15 MINUTES   10 MINUTES

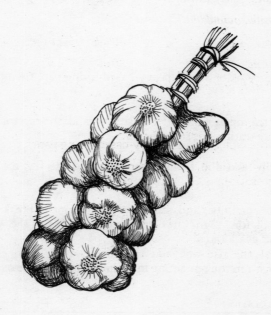

Creamy Cucumber Cod

SERVES 4	METRIC	IMPERIAL	AMERICAN
Oil	15 ml	1 tbsp	1 tbsp
Small shallot, finely chopped	1	1	1
Cod fillets, cut into strips 2.5 cm/1 in wide	450 g	1 lb	1 lb
Cucumber, peeled, seeded and very finely chopped	100 g	4 oz	4 oz
Greek-style natural yoghurt	30 ml	2 tbsp	2 tbsp
Double (heavy) cream	30 ml	2 tbsp	2 tbsp
Pinch of sugar			
Salt and freshly ground black pepper			

1   Heat the wok or a large heavy-based frying pan, then pour in the oil.

2   When the oil is hot add the shallot and stir-fry for about 1 minute until it has softened.

3   Carefully add the fish to the pan and stir-fry for about 2 minutes.

4   Add the cucumber and, still being careful not to break up the fish, cook for 1–2 minutes, ensuring that some of the water it gives off evaporates.

5   Gently stir in the remaining ingredients and heat through.

SERVING SUGGESTION

Serve with a selection of hot vegetables.

PREPARATION TIME:
10 MINUTES

COOKING TIME:
8 MINUTES

Orange Bass

SERVES 4	METRIC	IMPERIAL	AMERICAN
Oil	15 ml	1 tbsp	1 tbsp
Onion, finely chopped	1	1	1
Celery, finely sliced	100 g	4 oz	4 oz
Bass, skinned, boned and cut into chunks	350 g	12 oz	12 oz
Cornflour (cornstarch)	5 ml	1 tsp	1 tsp
Water	30 ml	2 tbsp	2 tbsp
Fresh orange juice	30 ml	2 tbsp	2 tbsp
Grated orange zest	10 ml	2 tsp	2 tsp
Salt and freshly ground black pepper			
Pinch of sugar			

1 Heat the wok or a large heavy-based frying pan.

2 Pour in the oil and when it is hot add the onion and celery and stir-fry for about 2 minutes or until both have softened slightly.

3 Add the bass to the pan and stir very carefully for about 1 minute.

4 Blend the cornflour with the water and add to the fish mixture with the orange juice and zest, seasoning and sugar.

5 Gently stir until the sauce has thickened slightly.

SERVING SUGGESTION

Serve hot with green vegetables and boiled new potatoes.

PREPARATION TIME: 15 MINUTES COOKING TIME: 6 MINUTES

Fish with Pasta in Tomato Sauce

SERVES 4	METRIC	IMPERIAL	AMERICAN
Oil	15 ml	1 tbsp	1 tbsp
Garlic cloves, crushed	2	2	2
Large onion, chopped	1	1	1
Medium red (bell) pepper, diced	1	1	1
Ripe tomatoes, skinned and chopped	4	4	4
Red wine	30 ml	2 tbsp	2 tbsp
Cod fillets, skinned, boned and cut into thick strips	350 g	12 oz	12 oz
Tomato purée (paste)	15 ml	1 tbsp	1 tbsp
Chopped fresh oregano	10 ml	2 tsp	2 tsp
Chopped fresh basil	5 ml	1 tsp	1 tsp
Precooked pasta shapes	75 g	3 oz	3 oz

1 Heat the wok or a large deep heavy-based frying pan.

2 Pour in the oil and when hot add the garlic and onion and stir-fry for about 1 minute.

3 Add the red pepper and cook for a further minute.

4 Stir in the tomatoes and wine and cook for 2–3 minutes.

5 Carefully stir in the remaining ingredients and cook for several minutes to cook the fish and ensure that the pasta is hot.

SERVING SUGGESTION

Serve hot with garlic bread.

PREPARATION TIME: **COOKING TIME:**
5 MINUTES **15 MINUTES**

Rapid Salmon

SERVES 4	METRIC	IMPERIAL	AMERICAN
Oil	15 ml	1 tbsp	1 tbsp
Garlic clove, crushed	1	1	1
Chopped fresh root ginger	5 ml	1 tsp	1 tsp
Finely chopped lemon grass	15 ml	1 tbsp	1 tbsp
Salmon fillet, cut into thick strips	350 g	12 oz	12 oz
Finely chopped fresh chives	30 ml	2 tbsp	2 tbsp
Lime juice	15 ml	1 tbsp	1 tbsp

1   Heat the wok or a large heavy-based frying pan.

2   Pour in the oil and when hot add the garlic and ginger and cook for 30 seconds.

3   Add the lemon grass and cook for a further 30 seconds.

4   Carefully add the salmon to the pan and gently stir-fry for about 1 minute only or the fish will break up.

5   Gently stir in the chives and serve with the lime juice drizzled over the top.

PREPARATION TIME:
10 MINUTES

COOKING TIME:
4 MINUTES

Creamy Cockles

SERVES 4	METRIC	IMPERIAL	AMERICAN
Oil	15 ml	1 tbsp	1 tbsp
Garlic cloves, finely chopped	2	2	2
Onion, finely chopped	1	1	1
Monkfish, cut into chunks	225 g	8 oz	8 oz
Sweet vermouth	60 ml	4 tbsp	4 tbsp
Cockles	225 g	8 oz	2 cups
Double (heavy) cream	150 ml	¼ pt	⅔ cup
Salt and freshly ground black pepper			

1   Heat the wok or a large heavy-based frying pan. Pour in the oil and heat.

2   Stir-fry the garlic and onion for about 1 minute.

3   Add the monkfish to the pan and stir carefully for about 2 minutes.

4   Pour in the vermouth, stir and cook the mixture for 2–3 minutes until the vermouth is reduced by half.

5   Stir in the cockles and cream and heat through. Season well.

SERVING SUGGESTION

Serve hot with creamed potatoes and hot vegetables.

PREPARATION TIME: COOKING TIME:
10 MINUTES   9 MINUTES

Prawns with Creamy Avocado Sauce

SERVES 4	METRIC	IMPERIAL	AMERICAN
Uncooked prawns (shrimp)	450 g	1 lb	2 cups
Avocado pear, peeled, stoned (pitted) and mashed	1	1	1
Lime juice	10 ml	2 tsp	2 tsp
Garlic cloves, crushed	2	2	2
Tomato purée (paste)	5 ml	1 tsp	1 tsp
Soured (dairy sour) cream	150 ml	¼ pt	⅔ cup
Pinch of cayenne pepper			
Pinch of salt			
Oil	15 ml	1 tbsp	1 tbsp
Spring onions (scallions), chopped	3	3	3
Chopped fresh parsley	10 ml	2 tsp	2 tsp

1 Peel and de-vein the prawns, then wash and dry.

2 Combine the mashed avocado with the lime juice, one of the garlic cloves, the tomato purée, soured cream, cayenne pepper and salt. Mix well to give a smooth sauce.

3 Heat the wok or a large heavy-based frying pan.

4 Pour in the oil and when hot stir-fry the remaining garlic and the spring onions for about 30 seconds.

5 Add the prawns and cook for a further minute.

6 Stir in the avocado sauce and cook, stirring, for about 2–3 minutes until the sauce is heated through but not boiling.

7 Serve hot, sprinkled with the parsley.

PREPARATION TIME:
25 MINUTES

COOKING TIME:
8 MINUTES

Indian Huss

SERVES 4	METRIC	IMPERIAL	AMERICAN
Huss	450 g	1 lb	1 lb
Oil	15 ml	1 tbsp	1 tbsp
Garlic clove, crushed	1	1	1
Chopped fresh root ginger	5 ml	1 tsp	1 tsp
Large onion, finely chopped	1	1	1
Curry powder	5 ml	1 tsp	1 tsp
Ground cumin	5 ml	1 tsp	1 tsp
Ground cinnamon	2.5 ml	½ tsp	½ tsp
Pinch of ground cloves			
Chilli powder	2.5 ml	½ tsp	½ tsp
Salt	2.5 ml	½ tsp	½ tsp
Pinch of sugar			
Water	30 ml	2 tbsp	2 tbsp
Natural yoghurt	150 ml	¼ pt	⅔ cup

1 Skin and bone the huss and cut the flesh into chunks.

2 Heat the wok or a large heavy-based frying pan.

3 Pour in the oil and when hot stir-fry the garlic, ginger and onion for about 1–2 minutes until the onion has softened.

4 Add the spices, salt and sugar and stir for about 30 seconds.

5 Add the fish and stir carefully so that it does not break up.

6 Stir in the water and yoghurt and cook for about 2 minutes or until fish is soft but not breaking up.

SERVING SUGGESTION

Serve hot with plain boiled rice and a side salad.

PREPARATION TIME: **COOKING TIME:**
10 MINUTES   **8 MINUTES**

Monkfish with Almonds

SERVES 4	METRIC	IMPERIAL	AMERICAN
Monkfish	450 g	1 lb	1 lb
Oil	30 ml	2 tbsp	2 tbsp
Garlic clove, crushed	1	1	1
Precooked, par-boiled new potatoes, sliced	175 g	6 oz	6 oz
Blanched whole almonds	75 g	3 oz	⅔ cup
Salt and freshly ground black pepper			
Chopped fresh dill (dill weed)	5 ml	1 tsp	1 tsp

1 Cut the monkfish into fairly thick strips 5 cm/2 in long.

2 Heat the wok or a large heavy-based frying pan.

3 Pour in the oil and when hot stir-fry the garlic for about 30 seconds.

4 Add the potatoes and almonds to the pan and cook, stirring, for about 1–2 minutes until the potatoes are golden at the edges.

5 Carefully add the monkfish and stir-fry gently for about 2 minutes, avoiding breaking up the fish.

6 Finally, sprinkle on plenty of salt and pepper and the dill. Give one last stir.

SERVING SUGGESTION

Serve piping hot with a crisp side salad.

PREPARATION TIME: COOKING TIME:
10 MINUTES   6 MINUTES

Lemon Fish Medley

SERVES 4	METRIC	IMPERIAL	AMERICAN
Cod	225 g	8 oz	8 oz
Salmon	225 g	8 oz	8 oz
Oil	30 ml	2 tbsp	2 tbsp
Mangetout (snow peas), trimmed	100 g	4 oz	4 oz
Lemon, grated rind and juice only	1	1	1
Salt and freshly ground black pepper			

1 Skin and bone the cod and the salmon and cut into thick strips.

2 Heat the wok or a large heavy-based frying pan.

3 Add the oil and when hot add the fish and mangetout, stirring gently to prevent the fish from breaking up. Cook for 1–2 minutes.

4 Stir through the lemon rind and juice and season.

SERVING SUGGESTION

Serve with new potatoes and a crisp green salad.

PREPARATION TIME:
10 MINUTES

COOKING TIME:
5 MINUTES

Fish Chow Mein

SERVES 4	METRIC	IMPERIAL	AMERICAN
Oil	15 ml	1 tbsp	1 tbsp
Garlic cloves, crushed	2	2	2
Spring onions (scallions), finely sliced	4	4	4
Mangetout (snow peas) trimmed	75 g	3 oz	3 oz
Cod fillets, fresh or thawed frozen, cut into thick strips	225 g	8 oz	8 oz
Dried egg noodles, cooked according to packet instructions and drained	225 g	8 oz	8 oz
Soy sauce	10 ml	2 tsp	2 tsp
Sugar	5 ml	1 tsp	1 tsp
Vinegar	5 ml	1 tsp	1 tsp
Sesame oil	5 ml	1 tsp	1 tsp
Cooked prawns (shrimp)	100 g	4 oz	1 cup

1   Heat the wok or a large heavy-based frying pan.

2   Pour in the oil and when hot add the garlic, onion and mangetout and stir-fry for about 1 minute.

3   Add the fish to the pan and carefully stir-fry for a further minute.

4   Stir in the noodles and all the remaining ingredients and continue to stir-fry for 2–3 minutes until the mixture is hot right through. Serve.

PREPARATION TIME: **COOKING TIME:**
10 MINUTES **6 MINUTES**

Cod with Smoked Mussels

SERVES 4	METRIC	IMPERIAL	AMERICAN
Oil	15 ml	1 tbsp	1 tbsp
Garlic cloves, crushed	2	2	2
Onion, chopped	1	1	1
Cod fillets, cut into 2.5 cm/1 in cubes	450 g	1 lb	1 lb
Large ripe tomatoes, skinned and chopped	4	4	4
Tomato purée (paste)	30 ml	2 tbsp	2 tbsp
Chopped fresh basil	30 ml	2 tbsp	2 tbsp
Fish or vegetable stock	150 ml	¼ pt	⅔ cup
Can smoked mussels, drained	85 g	3½ oz	1 small

1 Heat the wok or a large heavy-based frying pan.

2 Pour in the oil and when hot stir-fry the garlic and onion for 1 minute.

3 Add the fish to the pan and stir-fry carefully for about 1 minute.

4 Gently stir in the remaining ingredients and cook, stirring, for 3–4 minutes until the tomatoes are soft and pulpy.

SERVING SUGGESTION

Serve hot with buttered tagliatelle.

PREPARATION TIME:
10 MINUTES

COOKING TIME:
7 MINUTES

Sweet Fennel Monkfish

SERVES 4	METRIC	IMPERIAL	AMERICAN
Monkfish	450 g	1 lb	1 lb
Oil	15 ml	1 tbsp	1 tbsp
Shallots, finely sliced	2	2	2
Fennel heads, trimmed and green fronds reserved	3	3	3
Sweet cider	60 ml	4 tbsp	4 tbsp
Brown sugar	10 ml	2 tsp	2 tsp
Green peppercorns, crushed	5 ml	1 tsp	1 tsp
Pinch of salt			

1   Skin and bone the monkfish and cut into thick strips.

2   Heat the wok or a large heavy-based frying pan.

3   Pour in the oil and heat, then add the shallots and the fennel and stir-fry for about 4–5 minutes until the fennel is tender.

4   Add the monkfish to the pan and cook, stirring carefully, for about 1 minute.

5   Add the remaining ingredients and continue to cook for 2–3 minutes until fish is cooked but not breaking up.

6   Serve hot, garnished with the fennel fronds.

PREPARATION TIME:
10 MINUTES

COOKING TIME:
10 MINUTES

Crunchy Crab
with Chinese Leaves

SERVES 4	METRIC	IMPERIAL	AMERICAN
Oil	15 ml	1 tbsp	1 tbsp
French (green) beans, trimmed and cut into short lengths	50 g	2 oz	2 oz
Spring onions (scallions), chopped	5	5	5
Chinese leaves, finely shredded	100 g	4 oz	4 oz
Tinned water chestnuts drained and sliced	50 g	2 oz	2 oz
Cashew nuts	50 g	2 oz	½ cup
Fresh crabmeat	350 g	12 oz	12 oz
Soy sauce	15 ml	1 tbsp	1 tbsp
Oyster sauce	15 ml	1 tbsp	1 tbsp
Dry sherry	15 ml	1 tbsp	1 tbsp
Sugar	5 ml	1tsp	1 tsp
Cashew nuts, to garnish			

1   Heat the wok or a large heavy-based frying pan.

2   Pour in the oil and when hot add the beans, spring onions, Chinese leaves, water chestnuts and the measured cashew nuts and stir-fry for about 2 minutes.

3 Stir in the remaining ingredients except the extra cashew nuts and heat through.

4 Serve hot, sprinkled with a few cashew nuts.

PREPARATION TIME:
10 MINUTES

COOKING TIME:
5 MINUTES

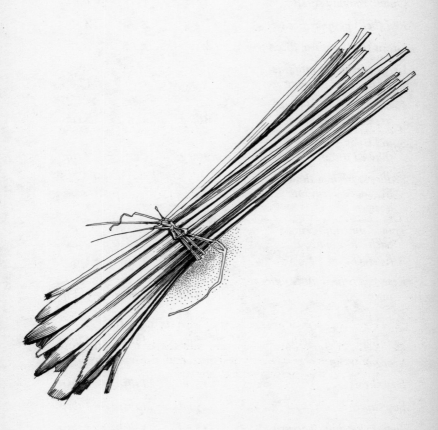

Sweet and Sour at Sea

SERVES 4	METRIC	IMPERIAL	AMERICAN
Oil	15 ml	1 tbsp	1 tbsp
Garlic clove, crushed	1	1	1
Chopped fresh root ginger	10 ml	2 tsp	2 tsp
Onion, roughly sliced	1	1	1
Red (bell) pepper, diced	½	½	½
Green (bell) pepper, diced	½	½	½
Large carrot, cut into fine sticks 5 cm/2 in long	1	1	1
Cooked prawns (shrimp) fresh or thawed frozen	100 g	4 oz	⅔ cup
Squid rings, fresh or thawed frozen	100 g	4 oz	⅔ cup
Scallops, fresh or thawed frozen, each cut into 4 slices	8	8	8
Tinned pineapple rings each cut into about 8 pieces	3	3	3
Reserved tinned pineapple juice	30 ml	2 tbsp	2 tbsp
Water	90 ml	6 tbsp	6 tbsp
Cornflour (cornstarch)	15 ml	1 tbsp	1 tbsp
Vinegar	10 ml	2 tsp	2 tsp
Dry sherry	15 ml	1 tbsp	1 tbsp
Soy sauce	15 ml	1 tbsp	1 tbsp
Tomato ketchup (catsup)	15 ml	1 tbsp	1 tbsp

1   Heat the wok or a large heavy-based frying pan.

2   Pour in the oil and when hot add the garlic and ginger and stir-fry for about 30 seconds.

3   Add the onion, red and green pepper and carrot and stir-fry for 2–3 minutes or until the vegetables are slightly softened.

4   Add all the shellfish and the pineapple to the pan and stir for 1 minute.

5   Mix together the pineapple juice, water and cornflour and when well blended mix in all the remaining ingredients.

6   Pour the cornflour mixture into the pan and stir well. Cook for 2–3 minutes, stirring continuously, until the sauce has thickened.

SERVING SUGGESTION

Serve with plain boiled rice

PREPARATION TIME:
15 MINUTES

COOKING TIME:
8 MINUTES

MEATY
MENUS

★

Mariner's Beef

SERVES 4	METRIC	IMPERIAL	AMERICAN
Oil	15 ml	1 tbsp	1 tbsp
Garlic clove, crushed	1	1	1
Spring onions (scallions), chopped	4	4	4
Beef, cut into thin strips	350 g	12 oz	12 oz
Cooked prawns (shrimp)	100 g	4 oz	½ cup
Scallops, fresh or thawed frozen, each cut into 4 slices	6	6	6
Salt and freshly ground black pepper			
Lemon juice	15 ml	1 tbsp	1 tbsp
Chopped fresh parsley	15 ml	1 tbsp	1 tbsp

1 Heat the wok or a large heavy-based frying pan.

2 Pour in the oil and when hot stir-fry the garlic and spring onions for about 30 seconds.

3 Add the beef to the pan and cook for 3–4 minutes or until it is tender.

4 Stir in the prawns and scallop slices and cook for 1 minute.

5 Season to taste, stir in the lemon juice and parsley and serve hot.

**PREPARATION TIME:
15 MINUTES**

**COOKING TIME:
8 MINUTES**

Spiced Chicken with Lentils and Green Chillis

SERVES 4	METRIC	IMPERIAL	AMERICAN
Oil	30 ml	2 tbsp	2 tbsp
Garlic cloves, crushed	2	2	2
Chopped fresh root ginger	15 ml	1 tbsp	1 tbsp
Cardamom pods	3	3	3
Whole mild green chillis, slit	8	8	8
Chicken breast, finely sliced	450 g	1 lb	1 lb
Precooked green lentils	100 g	4 oz	1 cup
Ground turmeric	2.5 ml	½ tsp	½ tsp
Ground cumin	2.5 ml	½ tsp	½ tsp
Salt	2.5 ml	½ tsp	½ tsp
Cherry tomatoes	12	12	12
Single (light) cream	150 ml	¼ pt	⅔ cup

1 Heat the wok or a large heavy-based frying pan.

2 Pour in the oil and when hot add the garlic, ginger and cardamom and stir-fry for a few seconds.

3 Add the chillis and chicken and cook for about 4 minutes.

4 Stir in the lentils and spices and cook for a few minutes.

5 Add the salt and tomatoes, stir-frying for 2 minutes.

6 Add the cream and heat through, stirring continuously.

SERVING SUGGESTION

Serve with boiled rice or Indian bread.

PREPARATION TIME:
10 MINUTES

COOKING TIME:
12 MINUTES

Kashmiri-style Lamb

SERVES 4	METRIC	IMPERIAL	AMERICAN
Oil	30 ml	2 tbsp	2 tbsp
Cumin seeds	5 ml	1 tsp	1 tsp
Cardamom pods, slightly crushed	4	4	4
Cloves, crushed	4	4	4
Onions, sliced	2	2	2
Garlic cloves, crushed	2	2	2
Chopped fresh root ginger	15 ml	1 tbsp	1 tbsp
Lean lamb, cut into fine strips	450 g	1 lb	1 lb
Chilli powder	5 ml	1 tsp	1 tsp
Ground cinnamon	5 ml	1 tsp	1 tsp
Medium-hot curry powder	5 ml	1 tsp	1 tsp
Salt	2.5 ml	½ tsp	½ tsp
Natural yoghurt	150 ml	¼ pt	⅔ cup

1 Heat the wok or a large heavy-based frying pan.

2 Add the oil, heat and then add the cumin seeds, cardamom and cloves and stir-fry for 30 seconds.

3 Add the onion, garlic and ginger and stir-fry until softened.

4 Add the lamb and stir-fry for about 3 minutes until it has changed colour.

5 Stir in the chilli powder, cinnamon, curry powder and salt.

6 Pour in the yoghurt, stir and heat through.

SERVING SUGGESTION

Serve with plain boiled rice.

PREPARATION TIME:
20 MINUTES

COOKING TIME:
10 MINUTES

Sausage with Baby Potatoes in Mustard Dressing

SERVES 4	METRIC	IMPERIAL	AMERICAN
Oil	30 ml	2 tbsp	2 tbsp
Garlic cloves, crushed	2	2	2
Large onion, sliced	1	1	1
Cooked sausage, e.g. Zywieska, salami smoked sausage ring, cut into bite-size chunks	350 g	12 oz	12 oz
Precooked baby new potatoes	225 g	8 oz	8 oz
Wholegrain mustard	30 ml	2 tbsp	2 tbsp
Honey	15 ml	1 tbsp	1 tbsp
Extra virgin olive oil	15 ml	1 tbsp	1 tbsp

Salt and freshly ground black pepper

1 Heat the wok or a large heavy-based frying pan.

2 Pour in the cooking oil and when hot add the garlic and cook for 30 seconds.

3 Add the onion and stir-fry for 1 minute.

4 Add the sausage and potatoes and stir-fry for 3–4 minutes to ensure that the mixture is heated through.

5 Combine the mustard, honey, olive oil and seasoning and pour into the pan.

6 Stir the mixture thoroughly and cook for a further minute.

SERVING SUGGESTION

Serve hot with a side salad.

PREPARATION TIME: 10 MINUTES

COOKING TIME: 8 MINUTES

Cranberry Turkey

SERVES 4	METRIC	IMPERIAL	AMERICAN
Turkey breast, sliced	450 g	1 lb	1 lb
Plain (all-purpose) flour	30 ml	2 tbsp	2 tbsp
Oil	30 ml	2 tbsp	2 tbsp
Onion, finely chopped	1	1	1
Fresh thyme sprigs	4	4	4
Cranberry jelly	60 ml	4 tbsp	4 tbsp
Port or sweet sherry	45 ml	3 tbsp	3 tbsp
Salt and freshly ground black pepper			

1 Dip the turkey in the flour.

2 Heat the wok or a large heavy-based frying pan.

3 Pour in the oil and when hot add the floured turkey, onion and thyme and stir-fry for about 3 minutes or until the turkey is tender.

4 Stir in the cranberry jelly and port or sherry. Season to taste.

5 Cook for several minutes until the sauce has thickened. If the sauce seems too thick, add a little water.

SERVING SUGGESTION

Serve hot with a selection of fresh vegetables.

PREPARATION TIME: **COOKING TIME:**
10 MINUTES   8 MINUTES

Maryland-style Chicken

SERVES 4	METRIC	IMPERIAL	AMERICAN
Cornflour (cornstarch)	10 ml	2 tsp	2 tsp
Cayenne pepper	2.5 ml	½ tsp	½ tsp
Water	5 ml	1 tsp	1 tsp
Worcestershire sauce	5 ml	1 tsp	1 tsp
Boneless chicken meat, cut into thin strips	450 g	1 lb	1 lb
Oil	30 ml	2 tbsp	2 tbsp
Baby sweetcorn (corn), fresh or thawed frozen	8	8	8
Bananas, sliced	2	2	2
Cashew nuts	15 ml	1 tbsp	1 tbsp

1 Combine the cornflour with the cayenne pepper, water and Worcestershire sauce and pour over the chicken. Marinate for 15 minutes.

2 Heat the wok or a large heavy-based frying pan.

3 Pour in the oil and when hot add the chicken and sweetcorn and stir-fry for about 4 minutes or until the chicken is tender.

4 Gently stir in the bananas and nuts and heat through.

SERVING SUGGESTION

Serve hot with a crisp salad.

PREPARATION TIME:
5 MINUTES PLUS
15 MINUTES
MARINATING TIME

COOKING TIME:
6 MINUTES

Boozy Beef

SERVES 4	METRIC	IMPERIAL	AMERICAN
Oil	30 ml	2 tbsp	2 tbsp
Large onion, sliced	1	1	1
Large carrot, very finely sliced	1	1	1
Celery sticks, finely sliced	2	2	2
Lean beef, cut into fine strips	450 g	1 lb	1 lb
Dried mixed herbs	2.5 ml	½ tsp	½ tsp
Wholegrain mustard	15 ml	1 tbsp	1 tbsp
Brown sugar	15 ml	1 tbsp	1 tbsp
Whisky	15–30 ml	1–2 tbsp	1–2 tbsp
Beef stock	300 ml	½ pt	1¼ cups
Cornflour (cornstarch)	10 ml	2 tsp	2 tsp

1 Heat the wok or a large heavy-based frying pan.

2 Pour in the oil and when hot add the onion, carrot and celery and stir-fry for about 2 minutes until slightly softened.

3 Add the beef and herbs and cook for 3 minutes or until tender.

4 Stir in the mustard, sugar, whisky and stock.

5 Cover the pan, reduce the heat and simmer for 5 minutes.

6 Blend the cornflour with a little water and stir into the pan.

7 Increase the heat and cook, stirring, until the gravy is slightly thickened.

SERVING SUGGESTION

Serve hot with warm bread.

PREPARATION TIME:
15 MINUTES

COOKING TIME:
15 MINUTES

Duck with Cherries

SERVES 4	METRIC	IMPERIAL	AMERICAN
Oil	30 ml	2 tbsp	2 tbsp
Shallots, finely chopped	2	2	2
Boneless duck meat, cut into fine strips	350 g	12 oz	12 oz
Can stoned (pitted) black cherries, drained and syrup reserved	410 g	14½ oz	1 large
Cornflour (cornstarch)	10 ml	2 tsp	2 tsp
Water	60 ml	4 tbsp	4 tbsp
Sweet sherry	15 ml	1 tbsp	1 tbsp

1   Heat the wok or a large heavy-based frying pan.

2   Pour in the oil and when hot stir-fry the shallots for about 1 minute.

3   Add the duck to the pan and stir-fry for 3–4 minutes or until tender.

4   Add the cherries and stir well.

5   Blend the cornflour with the water, then mix in the sherry and about 60 ml/4 tbsp of the reserved cherry syrup.

6   Pour into the pan and cook, stirring, for several minutes so that the sauce thickens.

SERVING SUGGESTION

Serve with a selection of hot vegetables.

PREPARATION TIME:
10 MINUTES

COOKING TIME:
10 MINUTES

Bengali-style Chicken

SERVES 4	METRIC	IMPERIAL	AMERICAN
Oil	30 ml	2 tbsp	2 tbsp
Garlic cloves, crushed	4	4	4
Chopped fresh root ginger	30 ml	2 tbsp	2 tbsp
Hot green chillis, finely diced	2	2	2
Large red onion, sliced	1	1	1
Boneless chicken meat, cut into strips	450 g	1 lb	1 lb
Large green (bell) pepper, sliced	1	1	1
Large ripe tomatoes, skinned and chopped	2	2	2
Pinch of sugar			
Salt	5 ml	1 tsp	1 tsp
Cayenne pepper	5 ml	1 tsp	1 tsp
Vinegar	15 ml	1 tbsp	1 tbsp

1   Heat the wok or a large heavy-based frying pan.

2   Pour in the oil and when hot add the garlic, ginger and chillis and cook for a few seconds.

3   Add the onion to the pan and cook for about 2 minutes or until it has softened slightly.

4   Stir in the chicken and cook for 3–4 minutes or until tender.

5   Add the green pepper and cook for about 30 seconds.

6   Add the remaining ingredients and stir for 3 minutes.

SERVING SUGGESTION

Serve hot with boiled rice.

PREPARATION TIME:
15 MINUTES

COOKING TIME:
12 MINUTES

Pork in Peanut Sauce

SERVES 4	METRIC	IMPERIAL	AMERICAN
Lean pork, very finely sliced into strips	225 g	8 oz	8 oz
Soy sauce	15 ml	1 tbsp	1 tbsp
Vinegar	15 ml	1 tbsp	1 tbsp
Sugar	5 ml	1 tsp	1 tsp
Five-spice powder	2.5 ml	½ tsp	½ tsp
Garlic cloves, crushed	2	2	2
Oil	30 ml	2 tbsp	2 tbsp
Onion, finely sliced	1	1	1
Carrot, cut into fine sticks	1	1	1
Large stick of celery, finely sliced	1	1	1
French (green) beans, cut into short lengths	25 g	1 oz	1 oz
Peanut butter	30 ml	2 tbsp	2 tbsp
Water	45 ml	3 tbsp	3 tbsp
Cornflour (cornstarch)	5 ml	1 tsp	1 tsp
Salted peanuts, roughly crushed	30 ml	2 tbsp	2 tbsp

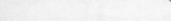

1   Combine the pork with the soy sauce, vinegar, sugar, spice and garlic and leave for about 10 minutes.

2   Heat the a wok or a large heavy-based frying pan.

3   Add the oil and when hot drop in the strips of pork reserving the marinade. Stir for a few minutes.

4 Add the onion, carrot, celery and beans and stir-fry until the meat is cooked and the vegetables slightly softened.

5 Mix in the marinade and the peanut butter.

6 Blend the cornflour with the cold water, then stir into the wok and continue to cook until the sauce has thickened.

7 Serve with peanuts sprinkled over the top.

PREPARATION TIME:
10 MINUTES PLUS
10 MINUTES
MARINATING TIME

COOKING TIME:
10 MINUTES

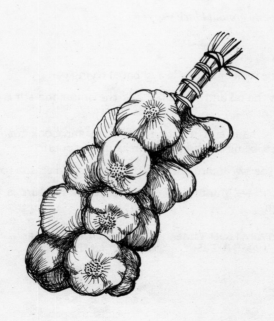

Ham Fry-up

SERVES 4	METRIC	IMPERIAL	AMERICAN
Oil	15 ml	1 tbsp	1 tbsp
Onion, finely chopped	1	1	1
Gammon ham, cut into small cubes	350 g	12 oz	1½ cups
Precooked potato, cut into small cubes	225 g	8 oz	8 oz
Canned or frozen sweetcorn (corn)	100 g	4 oz	1 cup
Cayenne pepper	2.5 ml	1 tsp	1 tsp

Salt and freshly ground black pepper

1   Heat the wok or a large heavy-based frying pan.

2   Pour in the oil and when hot add the onion and stir-fry for a minute.

3   Add the ham and potato to the pan and cook for several minutes, being careful not to break up the potato.

4   Stir in the sweetcorn and cayenne pepper and season to taste.

5   Cook for 1–2 minutes to ensure that the mixture is heated through.

PREPARATION TIME:
10 MINUTES

COOKING TIME:
6 MINUTES

Pork with Spinach

SERVES 4	METRIC	IMPERIAL	AMERICAN
Oil	30 ml	2 tbsp	2 tbsp
Garlic clove, crushed	1	1	1
Small onion, finely chopped	1	1	1
Boneless pork, cut into fine strips	450 g	1 lb	1 lb
Fresh spinach, finely chopped	350 g	12 oz	12 oz
Pinch of grated nutmeg			
Salt and freshly ground black pepper			
Soured (dairy sour) cream	150 ml	¼ pt	⅔ cup
Pine kernels, lightly toasted	25 g	1 oz	¼ cup

1   Heat the wok or a large heavy-based frying pan.

2   Pour in the oil and when hot add the garlic and onion and cook for about 30 seconds.

3   Add the pork and stir-fry for 3–4 minutes or until the meat is tender.

4   Stir in the spinach and cook for 30–60 seconds until it is wilted.

5   Add the nutmeg, season to taste, then stir in the cream. Heat through.

6   Serve garnished with the toasted pine kernels.

PREPARATION TIME: **COOKING TIME:**
15 MINUTES **8 MINUTES**

Kidneys in Sherry

SERVES 4	METRIC	IMPERIAL	AMERICAN
Lambs' kidneys	12	12	12
Plain (all-purpose) flour	30 ml	2 tbsp	2 tbsp
Oil	15 ml	1 tbsp	1 tbsp
Small onion, chopped	1	1	1
Button mushrooms, quartered	50 g	2 oz	2 oz
Beef stock	300 ml	½ pt	1¼ cups
Sweet sherry	60 ml	4 tbsp	4 tbsp
Redcurrant jelly (clear conserve)	15 ml	1 tbsp	1 tbsp

Salt and freshly ground black pepper

1   Skin and core the kidneys and cut each into four pieces.

2   Coat each piece with the flour.

3   Heat a wok or large heavy-based frying pan.

4   Pour in the oil and when hot cook the onion for 1 minute.

5   Add the kidneys and mushrooms and stir-fry for 3–4 minutes or until the juices run clear.

6   Stir in any remaining flour, then gradually blend in the stock and sherry.

7   Cook, stirring, for several minutes so that the sherry sauce thickens slightly.

8   Stir in the redcurrant jelly until it is dissolved. Season to taste.

SERVING SUGGESTION

Serve hot with buttered noodles.

PREPARATION TIME: **COOKING TIME:**
15 MINUTES　　　　**10 MINUTES**

Turkey with Noodles

SERVES 4	METRIC	IMPERIAL	AMERICAN
Turkey breast, cut into thin slices	350 g	12 oz	12 oz
Plain (all-purpose) flour, seasoned	30 ml	2 tbsp	2 tbsp
Oil	15 ml	1 tbsp	1 tbsp
Small shallots, finely chopped	2	2	2
Button mushrooms, sliced	100 g	4 oz	4 oz
Chopped fresh thyme	10 ml	2 tsp	2 tsp
Dry vermouth	45 ml	3 tbsp	3 tbsp
Single (light) cream	150 ml	¼ pt	⅔ cup
Salt and freshly ground black pepper			
Cooked green tagliatelle	100 g	4 oz	4 oz

1   Coat the turkey in the seasoned flour. Heat the wok or a large heavy-based frying pan.

2   Add the oil and when hot put the turkey and shallots in the pan and cook for 3–4 minutes until the meat is tender.

3   Add the mushrooms and thyme and cook for 1 minute.

4   Sprinkle any remaining flour over the surface of the contents of the pan and stir in well.

5   Gradually blend in the vermouth and cream and cook, stirring, until the sauce is slightly thickened.

6   Season to taste, then stir in the tagliatelle and ensure that the mixture is heated through.

SERVING SUGGESTION

Serve hot with a crisp salad.

PREPARATION TIME: **COOKING TIME:**
10 MINUTES   **10 MINUTES**

Sausage Supper

SERVES 4	METRIC	IMPERIAL	AMERICAN
Oil	30 ml	2 tbsp	2 tbsp
Garlic clove, crushed	1	1	1
Large onion, sliced	1	1	1
Herby chipolatas, cut into chunks	450 g	1 lb	1 lb
Red (bell) pepper, diced	½	½	½
Celery stick, finely chopped	1	1	1
Mushrooms, sliced	50 g	2 oz	2 oz
Precooked green lentils	50 g	2 oz	½ cup
Chilli powder	2.5 ml	½ tsp	½ tsp
Mixed dried herbs	5 ml	1 tsp	1 tsp
Tomato purée (paste)	15 ml	1 tbsp	1 tbsp
Can chopped tomatoes	400 g	14 oz	1 large
Salt and freshly ground black pepper			

1   Heat the wok or a large heavy-based frying pan.

2   Pour in the oil and when hot stir-fry the garlic and onion for about 1 minute.

3   Add the chipolatas and stir carefully for about 2 minutes until they are well browned.

4   Add the pepper, celery and mushrooms and cook for 1 minute.

5   Add the remaining ingredients, cover and simmer for 5 minutes.

SERVING SUGGESTION

Serve hot with crusty bread.

PREPARATION TIME: **COOKING TIME:**
15 MINUTES **12 MINUTES**

Lamb with Apricots

SERVES 4	METRIC	IMPERIAL	AMERICAN
Boneless lamb, cut into fine strips	450 g	1 lb	1 lb
Plain (all-purpose) flour, seasoned	30 ml	2 tbsp	2 tbsp
Oil	30 ml	2 tbsp	2 tbsp
Shallot, finely chopped	1	1	1
Can apricot halves, drained	410 g	14½ oz	1 large
Salt and freshly ground black pepper			
Flaked almonds, lightly toasted	25 g	1 oz	¼ cup

1 Coat the pieces of lamb in the seasoned flour.

2 Heat the wok or a large heavy-based frying pan.

3 Pour in the oil and when hot add the shallot and cook for about 30 seconds.

4 Add the lamb to the pan and stir-fry for 4–5 minutes until it is tender and a little crisp.

5 Stir in the apricot halves and season to taste, then cook for several minutes until it is heated through.

6 Serve hot with the toasted almonds sprinkled over the surface.

PREPARATION TIME: 5 MINUTES COOKING TIME: 9 MINUTES

Chicken in Asparagus Sauce

SERVES 4	METRIC	IMPERIAL	AMERICAN
Oil	*15 ml*	*1 tbsp*	*1 tbsp*
Small onion, finely chopped	*1*	*1*	*1*
Boneless chicken meat, cut into fine strips	*450 g*	*1 lb*	*1 lb*
Button mushrooms, quartered	*50 g*	*2 oz*	*2 oz*
Can condensed asparagus soup	*295 g*	*11 oz*	*1 medium*
Canned asparagus spears, cut into short lengths	*8*	*8*	*8*
Salt and freshly ground black pepper			

1 Heat the wok or a large heavy-based frying pan.

2 Pour in the oil and stir-fry the onion and chicken for 3–4 minutes or until the meat is tender.

3 Add the mushrooms and cook for a further minute.

4 Gently stir in the undiluted soup and asparagus pieces.

5 Heat through and then season to taste.

SERVING SUGGESTION

Serve hot with a selection of hot baby new vegetables.

PREPARATION TIME:
10 MINUTES

COOKING TIME:
10 MINUTES

Lambs' Liver with Barbecue Sauce

SERVES 4	METRIC	IMPERIAL	AMERICAN
Oil	15 ml	1 tbsp	1 tbsp
Garlic cloves, crushed	2	2	2
Onion, finely chopped	1	1	1
Small red (bell) pepper, cut into thin strips	1	1	1
Lambs' liver, cut into thin strips	350 g	12 oz	12 oz
Tomato purée (paste)	5 ml	1 tsp	1 tsp
Vinegar	30 ml	2 tbsp	2 tbsp
Brown sugar	15 ml	1 tbsp	1 tbsp
Honey	15 ml	1 tbsp	1 tbsp
Mustard powder	5 ml	1 tsp	1 tsp
Chilli powder	2.5 ml	½ tsp	½ tsp
Water	150 ml	¼ pt	⅔ cup

1 Heat the wok or a large heavy-based frying pan.

2 Pour in the oil and when hot stir-fry the garlic for 30 seconds.

3 Add the onion and pepper and cook for a minute.

4 Add the liver to the pan and fry for about 3 minutes or until the juices are no longer bloody.

5 Stir in all the remaining ingredients and cook, stirring, for a further 3 minutes.

SERVING SUGGESTION

Serve hot with boiled rice.

PREPARATION TIME: **COOKING TIME:**
10 MINUTES **9 MINUTES**

Crunchy Chicken Stir-fry

SERVES 4	METRIC	IMPERIAL	AMERICAN
Oil	15 ml	1 tbsp	1 tbsp
Garlic clove, crushed	1	1	1
Chopped fresh root ginger	5 ml	1 tsp	1 tsp
Spring onions (scallions), cut into short lengths	4	4	4
Boneless chicken meat, cut into thin strips	350 g	12 oz	12 oz
Mangetout (snow peas)	50 g	2 oz	2 oz
French (green) beans, cut into short lengths	50 g	2 oz	2 oz
Bamboo shoots, thinly sliced	50 g	2 oz	2 oz
Cashew nuts	50 g	2 oz	½ cup
Pinch of salt			
Pinch of sugar			
Soy sauce	15 ml	1 tbsp	1 tbsp
Sesame oil	10 ml	2 tsp	2 tsp

1 Heat the wok or a large heavy-based frying pan.

2 Pour in the oil and when hot add the garlic, ginger and spring onions and stir-fry for about 30 seconds.

3 Add the chicken and cook for about 3 minutes until tender.

4 Stir in the mangetout, beans and bamboo shoots and cook for a minute.

5 Add the remaining ingredients and stir for 1–2 minutes to ensure that the mixture is hot throughout.

PREPARATION TIME: 15 MINUTES   **COOKING TIME:** 8 MINUTES

Sagey Pork

SERVES 4	METRIC	IMPERIAL	AMERICAN
Oil	30 ml	2 tbsp	2 tbsp
Large onion, sliced	1	1	1
Boneless pork, cut into fine strips	450 g	1 lb	1 lb
Plain (all-purpose) flour, seasoned	30 ml	2 tbsp	2 tbsp
Chopped fresh sage	15 ml	1 tbsp	1 tbsp
Can butter beans, drained	200 g	7 oz	1 small
Meat or vegetable stock	60 ml	4 tbsp	4 tbsp
Salt and freshly ground black pepper			

1 Heat the wok or a large heavy-based frying pan.

2 Pour in the oil and heat, then add the onion and stir-fry for about a minute.

3 Dip the pork in the seasoned flour, then add to the pan and cook for 3–4 minutes to tenderise the meat.

4 Stir in the sage and cook for a further minute.

5 Stir in the beans and heat through.

6 Pour in the stock and season to taste, then cook, stirring, for several minutes to thicken the gravy slightly.

SERVING SUGGESTION

Serve with creamed or jacket potatoes.

PREPARATION TIME:	COOKING TIME:
10 MINUTES	10 MINUTES

Hot Bacon

SERVES 4	METRIC	IMPERIAL	AMERICAN
Oil	*15 ml*	*1 tbsp*	*1 tbsp*
Garlic cloves, crushed	*2*	*2*	*2*
Small hot red chilli, very finely chopped	*1*	*1*	*1*
Large onion, finely sliced	*1*	*1*	*1*
Thick smoked bacon, cubed	*350 g*	*12 oz*	*12 oz*
Red (bell) pepper, cut into thin slices	*1*	*1*	*1*
Green (bell) pepper, cut into thin slices	*1*	*1*	*1*
Pinch of salt			
For the topping:			
Thick white bread slices, cut into 1 cm/½ in cubes	*2*	*2*	*2*
Chilli powder	*5 ml*	*1 tsp*	*1 tsp*
Oil	*30 ml*	*2 tbsp*	*2 tbsp*

1   Heat the wok or a large heavy-based frying pan.

2   Pour in the oil and when hot stir-fry the garlic and chilli for a few seconds.

3   Add the onion, bacon and sliced peppers and cook for about 3 minutes until the bacon has changed colour and the onion softened.

4   Stir in the salt, then transfer the mixture from the pan to another dish and keep hot.

5   Toss the bread cubes in the chilli powder.

6 Reheat the wok or frying pan and pour in the oil.

7 When the oil is very hot, drop in the bread cubes and stir-fry until they are tinged brown and slightly crisp.

8 Scatter the fried bread cubes over the bacon mixture.

SERVING SUGGESTION

Serve hot with a side salad.

PREPARATION TIME: COOKING TIME:
15 MINUTES   8 MINUTES

Rosemary Lamb

SERVES 4	METRIC	IMPERIAL	AMERICAN
Oil	*30 ml*	*2 tbsp*	*2 tbsp*
Garlic clove, crushed	*1*	*1*	*1*
Large red onion, roughly sliced	*1*	*1*	*1*
Chopped fresh rosemary	*10 ml*	*2 tsp*	*2 tsp*
Boneless lamb, cut into fine strips	*450 g*	*1 lb*	*1 lb*
Redcurrant jelly (clear conserve)	*30 ml*	*2 tbsp*	*2 tbsp*
Stock	*45 ml*	*3 tbsp*	*3 tbsp*
Red wine	*30 ml*	*2 tbsp*	*2 tbsp*
Salt and freshly ground black pepper			
Fresh rosemary sprigs	*4*	*4*	*4*

1 Heat the wok or a large heavy-based frying pan.

2 Pour in the oil and when hot add the garlic and onion and cook for a minute

3 Stir in the chopped rosemary and the lamb and cook for about 3–4 minutes or until the meat is tender.

4 Add the jelly, stock and wine. Season to taste and cook for about 2 minutes.

5 Serve hot, garnished with the rosemary sprigs.

PREPARATION TIME: COOKING TIME:
10 MINUTES   9 MINUTES

Turkey with Leeks

SERVES 4	METRIC	IMPERIAL	AMERICAN
Oil	30 ml	2 tbsp	2 tbsp
Leeks, finely sliced	2	2	2
Shallot, finely chopped	1	1	1
Turkey breast, finely sliced	450 g	1 lb	1 lb
Plain (all-purpose) flour, seasoned	30 ml	2 tbsp	2 tbsp
Chicken stock	60 ml	4 tbsp	4 tbsp
Single (light) cream	150 ml	¼ pt	⅔ cup
Cheddar cheese, grated	50 g	2 oz	½ cup
Pinch of grated nutmeg			
Salt and freshly ground black pepper			

1   Heat the wok or a large heavy-based frying pan.

2   Pour in the oil and heat, then add the leeks and shallot and stir-fry for about 2 minutes or until they are softened.

3   Dip the turkey strips in the seasoned flour, then add to the pan and cook for 3–4 minutes to tenderise the meat.

4   Pour in the stock and cream and cook, stirring constantly, until the sauce is slightly thickened.

5   Add the cheese and stir the mixture until it melts.

6   Season to taste and add the nutmeg.

7   Serve hot.

PREPARATION TIME:
10 MINUTES

COOKING TIME:
10 MINUTES

Spicy Chicken Livers

SERVES 4	METRIC	IMPERIAL	AMERICAN
Plain (all-purpose) flour	15 ml	1 tbsp	1 tbsp
Chilli powder	5 ml	1 tsp	1 tsp
Cumin	2.5 ml	½ tsp	½ tsp
Curry powder	2.5 ml	½ tsp	½ tsp
Salt and freshly ground black pepper			
Chicken livers, sliced	450 g	1 lb	2 cups
Oil	30 ml	2 tbsp	2 tbsp
Garlic cloves, crushed	2	2	2
Shallot, finely chopped	1	1	1
Small red chilli, very finely chopped	1	1	1
Chopped fresh coriander (cilantro)	15 ml	1 tbsp	1 tbsp

1   Combine the flour, spices and salt and freshly ground black pepper and use to coat the chicken livers.

2   Heat the wok or a large heavy-based frying pan.

3   Pour in the oil and when very hot add the garlic, shallot and chilli and stir-fry for about 30 seconds.

4   Add the chicken livers to the pan and carefully stir-fry them for 2–3 minutes until they are crisp on the outside and the juices are no longer bloody.

5   Serve hot sprinkled with the fresh coriander.

PREPARATION TIME: 10 MINUTES **COOKING TIME: 5 MINUTES**

Gammon with Peaches

SERVES 4	METRIC	IMPERIAL	AMERICAN
Oil	15 ml	1 tbsp	1 tbsp
Gammon steaks, cut in 2.5cm/1 in cubes	450 g	1 lb	1 lb
Can peach slices, syrup retained	410 g	14½ oz	1 large
Mustard powder	5 ml	1 tsp	1 tsp
Paprika	2.5 ml	½ tsp	½ tsp
Cornflour (cornstarch)	5 ml	1 tsp	1 tsp
Salt and freshly ground black pepper			

1 Heat the wok or a large heavy-based frying pan.

2 Pour in the oil and when hot add the gammon and stir-fry for 3–4 minutes or until the meat is tender.

3 Stir in the peaches.

4 Combine the reserved peach syrup with water to make up to 90 ml/6 tbsp, then blend in the mustard powder, paprika and cornflour.

5 Pour the syrup mixture into the pan and cook, stirring for 1–2 minutes so that the sauce is slightly thickened.

6 Season to taste and serve hot.

PREPARATION TIME: 5 MINUTES COOKING TIME: 7 MINUTES

Rabbit with Prunes

SERVES 4	METRIC	IMPERIAL	AMERICAN
Boneless rabbit, cut into strips	350 g	12 oz	12 oz
Plain (all-purpose) flour, seasoned	30 ml	2 tbsp	2 tbsp
Oil	30 ml	2 tbsp	2 tbsp
Garlic cloves, thinly sliced	3	3	3
Shallots, quartered	8	8	8
Celery stick, sliced	1	1	1
Dried stoned (pitted) prunes, soaked and halved	8	8	8
Green peppercorns, crushed	5 ml	1 tsp	1 tsp
Chicken stock	300 ml	½ pt	1¼ cups
Salt			

1   Coat the rabbit with the flour.

2   Heat the wok or a large heavy-based frying pan.

3   Pour in the oil and heat, then add the garlic, shallots and celery and cook for about 1–2 minutes until slightly softened.

4   Add the rabbit to the pan and stir-fry until it is tender, probably about 3 minutes.

5   Stir in the prunes and peppercorns with any remaining flour.

6   Gradually blend in the stock, bring to the boil and cook, stirring until the gravy is slightly thickened. Add salt to taste.

SERVING SUGGESTION

Serve with hot vegetables.

**PREPARATION TIME:
5 MINUTES PLUS SOAKING
TIME FOR THE PRUNES**

**COOKING TIME:
10 MINUTES**

Chicken with Artichoke Hearts

SERVES 4	METRIC	IMPERIAL	AMERICAN
Oil	30 ml	2 tbsp	2 tbsp
Garlic clove, crushed	1	1	1
Small onion, finely chopped	1	1	1
Boneless chicken meat, thinly sliced	450 g	1 lb	1 lb
Mushrooms, quartered	100 g	4 oz	4 oz
Can artichoke hearts, drained	400 g	14 oz	1 large
Balsamic vinegar or red wine vinegar	15 ml	1 tbsp	1 tbsp
Brown sugar	10 ml	2 tsp	2 tsp
Lemon juice	5 ml	1 tsp	1 tsp
Salt and freshly ground black pepper			

1 Heat the wok or a large heavy-based frying pan.

2 Pour in the oil and when hot stir-fry the garlic and onion for about 30 seconds.

3 Add the chicken to the pan and cook for 3 minutes or until tender.

4 Add the mushrooms and cook for a further minute.

5 Carefully stir in the remaining ingredients and avoid breaking up the artichoke hearts, then cook for several minutes to heat the mixture thoroughly.

6 Serve hot.

PREPARATION TIME: **COOKING TIME:**
10 MINUTES   8 MINUTES

Special Stir-fried Pork

SERVES 4	METRIC	IMPERIAL	AMERICAN
Oil	30 ml	2 tbsp	2 tbsp
Garlic clove, crushed	1	1	1
Chopped fresh root ginger	10 ml	2 tsp	2 tsp
Mild fresh green chilli, finely diced	1	1	1
Baby new carrots, halved lengthways	6	6	6
Spring onions (scallions), cut into short lengths	4	4	4
Mangetout (snow peas), trimmed	50 g	2 oz	2 oz
Baby sweetcorn (corn), fresh or thawed frozen	8	8	8
Boneless pork, cut into fine strips	350 g	12 oz	12 oz
Bean sprouts	50 g	2 oz	2 oz
Sweet chilli sauce	15 ml	1 tbsp	1 tbsp
Soy sauce	10 ml	2 tsp	2 tsp
Vinegar	5 ml	1 tsp	1 tsp
Pinch of sugar			

1 Heat the wok or a large heavy-based frying pan.

2 Pour in the oil and when hot stir-fry the garlic, ginger and chilli for 30 seconds.

3 Add the carrots and stir-fry for 1–2 minutes so that they start to soften slightly.

4 Add the onions, mangetout and sweetcorn and cook for 30 seconds.

5 Stir in the pork and cook for 3–4 minutes or until it is tender.

6 Carefully stir in the bean sprouts and all the remaining ingredients.

7 Heat through, giving a final few stirs.

SERVING SUGGESTION

Serve hot with boiled rice

PREPARATION TIME:
15 MINUTES

COOKING TIME:
10 MINUTES

Juniper Venison

SERVES 4	METRIC	IMPERIAL	AMERICAN
Oil	15 ml	1 tbsp	1 tbsp
Garlic cloves, finely sliced	3	3	3
Shallots, quartered	8	8	8
Celery sticks, finely sliced	2	2	2
Boneless venison meat, cut into fine strips	350 g	12 oz	12 oz
Plain (all-purpose) flour, seasoned	30 ml	2 tbsp	2 tbsp
Juniper berries, crushed	10 ml	2 tsp	2 tsp
Green peppercorns, crushed	5 ml	1 tsp	1 tsp
Finely grated orange rind	5 ml	1 tsp	1 tsp
Orange juice	30 ml	2 tbsp	2 tbsp
Beef stock	300 ml	½ pt	1¼ cups
Salt			

1 Heat the wok or a large heavy-based frying pan.

2 Pour in the oil and when hot stir-fry the garlic and shallots for about 1 minute.

3 Add the celery to the pan and cook for a further minute.

4 Dip the venison quickly in the seasoned flour and add to the pan, stir-frying for 3–4 minutes or until the meat is tender.

5 Stir in the juniper berries, peppercorns and orange zest and cook for a few seconds.

6 Sprinkle any remaining flour over the meat mixture and stir it in.

7 Stirring constantly, gradually blend in the orange juice and beef stock. Cook for a few minutes to thicken the gravy slightly and add salt to taste.

SERVING SUGGESTION

Serve hot with roast potatoes and vegetables.

PREPARATION TIME: **COOKING TIME:**
15 MINUTES **10 MINUTES**

Chicken with Olives

SERVES 4	METRIC	IMPERIAL	AMERICAN
Oil	30 ml	2 tbsp	2 tbsp
Garlic cloves, crushed	4	4	4
Very small shallots or small pickling onions, halved	175 g	6 oz	1½ cups
Chicken breast, cut into fine strips	450 g	1 lb	1 lb
Mushrooms, quartered	100 g	4 oz	4 oz
White wine	150 ml	¼ pt	⅔ cup
Black olives, pitted (stoned)	100 g	4 oz	⅔ cup
Single (light) cream	30 ml	2 tbsp	2 tbsp
Salt and freshly ground black pepper			

1 Heat the wok or a large heavy-based frying pan.

2 Pour in the oil and when hot stir-fry the garlic for about 30 seconds.

3 Add the onions to the pan and stir-fry for about 3–4 minutes so they are quite soft.

4 Add the chicken and cook for 3 minutes or until tender.

5 Stir in the mushrooms and cook for another minute.

6 Pour in the wine and olives, bring the mixture to the boil and continue cooking for a minute or so to reduce the liquid.

7 Finally, stir in the cream, season and heat through.

SERVING SUGGESTION

Serve hot with buttered noodles.

PREPARATION TIME: **COOKING TIME:**
15 MINUTES **15 MINUTES**

Peking-style Duck

SERVES 4	METRIC	IMPERIAL	AMERICAN
Soy sauce	10 ml	2 tsp	2 tsp
Dry sherry	10 ml	2 tsp	2 tsp
Pinch of five-spice powder			
Boneless duck meat, cut into thin strips	450 g	1 lb	1 lb
Oil	30 ml	2 tbsp	2 tbsp
Garlic clove, crushed	1	1	1
Spring onions (scallions), finely shredded	4	4	4
Cucumber, peeled, seeded and cut into short sticks	50 g	2 oz	2 oz
Hoisin sauce	30 ml	2 tbsp	2 tbsp

1 Combine the soy sauce, sherry and five-spice powder and use to marinate the duck for 15 minutes.

2 Heat the wok or a large heavy-based frying pan.

3 Pour in the oil and when hot add the garlic and stir-fry for 30 seconds.

4 Add the duck and cook for about 3 minutes or until tender.

5 Add the spring onions and cucumber and cook for 1 minute.

6 Stir in the hoisin sauce and the remaining marinade and heat the duck mixture through thoroughly.

SERVING SUGGESTION

Serve hot with rice or Chinese pancakes.

PREPARATION TIME:
10 MINUTES PLUS
15 MINUTES
MARINATING TIME

COOKING TIME:
7 MINUTES

Summer Lamb

SERVES 4	METRIC	IMPERIAL	AMERICAN
Baby carrots, scrubbed, topped and tailed	100 g	4 oz	4 oz
Baby courgettes (zucchini), trimmed	100 g	4 oz	4 oz
Baby new potatoes, scrubbed	100 g	4 oz	4 oz
Oil	30 ml	2 tbsp	2 tbsp
Baby shallots, halved	8	8	8
Minced (ground) lamb	450 g	1 lb	2 cups
Mint jelly	30 ml	2 tbsp	2 tbsp
Lamb or beef stock	150 ml	¼ pt	⅔ cup
Frozen peas	50 g	2 oz	½ cup
Salt and freshly ground black pepper			
Fresh mint sprigs	4	4	4

1 Bring a saucepan of water to the boil, then put in the carrots and potatoes and cook for about 3 minutes.

2 Add the courgettes to the boiling water and cook for a further 2 minutes.

3 Drain the vegetables well.

4 Heat the wok or a large heavy-based frying pan.

5 Pour in the oil and when hot add the shallots and stir-fry for about 3 minutes or until they start to soften.

6 Add the lamb to the pan and cook for 3–4 minutes or until well browned.

7 Add the baby vegetables to the pan and stir. Cook for 2 minutes.

8 Finally, stir in the mint jelly, stock and peas, then season to taste and heat through.

9 Serve garnished with the mint sprigs.

PREPARATION TIME: 10 MINUTES COOKING TIME: 15 MINUTES

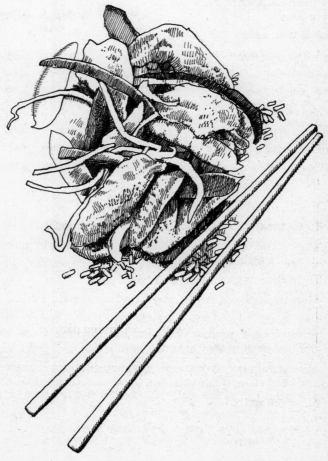

Mini Chicken Meatballs

SERVES 4	METRIC	IMPERIAL	AMERICAN
Cooked chicken meat, finely minced (ground)	350 g	12 oz	1½ cups
Garlic cloves, crushed	2	2	2
Small onion, finely grated or minced (ground)	1	1	1
Very finely chopped fresh root ginger	15 ml	1 tbsp	1 tbsp
Pinch of fenugreek			
Pinch of ground cinnamon			
Ground cumin	2.5 ml	½ tsp	½ tsp
Chilli powder	2.5 ml	½ tsp	½ tsp
Ground cloves	2.5 ml	½ tsp	½ tsp
Salt	1.5 ml	¼ tsp	¼ tsp
Natural yoghurt	5–10 ml	1–2 tsp	1–2 tsp
Oil	60 ml	4 tbsp	4 tbsp

1 Combine the chicken, garlic, onion, spices and salt.

2 Stir in 5 ml/1 tsp of the yoghurt and if the mixture seems too dry add a little more to bind it.

3 Form the mixture into walnut-sized balls.

4 Heat the wok or a large heavy-based frying pan.

5 Pour in the oil and when very hot fry (sauté) the meatballs a few at a time, stirring very gently all the time. Cook for 2–3 minutes or until they are browned all over.

6 Lift the balls out with a draining spoon, place on kitchen paper and keep warm while you cook the remaining meatballs.

7 Serve hot or cold.

PREPARATION TIME: **COOKING TIME:**
10 MINUTES 10 MINUTES

Autumn Pork

SERVES 4	METRIC	IMPERIAL	AMERICAN
Oil	15 ml	1 tbsp	1 tbsp
Large onion, finely chopped	1	1	1
Garlic clove, crushed	1	1	1
Minced (ground) pork	450 g	1 lb	4 cups
Mushrooms, quartered	100 g	4 oz	4 oz
Large eating (dessert) apple, peeled, cored and cubed	1	1	1
Medium-dry cider	150 ml	¼ pt	⅔ cup
Apple chutney	30 ml	2 tbsp	2 tbsp
Ground mace	2.5 ml	½ tsp	½ tsp
Salt and freshly ground black pepper			
Potatoes, diced and par-boiled until just tender	450 g	1 lb	1 lb

❖

1 Heat the wok or a large heavy-based frying pan. Add the oil.

2 When hot add the onion and garlic and stir-fry for 1 minute.

3 Add the pork and cook, stirring, for about 2 minutes or until all the meat has changed colour.

4 Stir in the mushrooms and apple cubes and cook for 2–3 minutes so that both have softened slightly.

5 Add the cider, chutney, mace, salt and freshly ground black pepper. Stir for a further minute.

6 Gently mix in the cooked potato, heat through and serve.

PREPARATION TIME: **COOKING TIME:**
10 MINUTES **11 MINUTES**

Turkey in Damson Sauce

SERVES 4	METRIC	IMPERIAL	AMERICAN
Oil	15 ml	1 tbsp	1 tbsp
Garlic clove, crushed	1	1	1
Large red onion, chopped	1	1	1
Boneless turkey meat, cut into fine strips	450 g	1 lb	1 lb
Damson jam (jelly)	45 ml	3 tbsp	3 tbsp
Chicken stock	125 ml	¼ pt	⅔ cup
Salt and freshly ground black pepper			

1   Heat the wok or a large heavy-based frying pan.

2   Pour in the oil and when hot add the garlic and onion and cook for about 1 minute.

3   Add the turkey to the pan and stir-fry for several minutes until tender.

4   Stir in the jam and stock and boil to reduce the volume of liquid slightly and produce a syrupy sauce. Season to taste.

SERVING SUGGESTION

Serve with fresh vegetables.

PREPARATION TIME:
10 MINUTES

COOKING TIME:
8 MINUTES

'Woky' Coq au Vin

SERVES 4	METRIC	IMPERIAL	AMERICAN
Oil	30 ml	2 tbsp	2 tbsp
Garlic cloves, crushed	2	2	2
Small shallots, halved	100 g	4 oz	4 oz
Boneless chicken meat, sliced	450 g	1 lb	1 lb
Smoked bacon, cubed	100 g	4 oz	4 oz
Small button mushrooms	100 g	4 oz	4 oz
Thyme sprig	1	1	1
Dried parsley	5 ml	1 tsp	1 tsp
Bay leaves	2	2	2
Red wine	125 ml	¼ pt	⅔ cup
Chicken stock	125 ml	¼ pt	⅔ cup

Salt and freshly ground black pepper

1   Heat the wok or a large heavy-based frying pan.

2   Pour in the oil and when hot add the garlic and shallots and stir-fry for several minutes until slightly tender.

3   Add the chicken and bacon and cook for a further 3–4 minutes or until the meat is tender.

4   Stir in the mushrooms and herbs and cook for several minutes.

5   Add the wine and stock and bring to the boil.

6   Cover the pan, reduce to a simmer and cook for about 15 minutes, stirring occasionally. Season to taste and serve hot.

SERVING SUGGESTION

Serve with a selection of seasonal vegetables.

PREPARATION TIME: **COOKING TIME:**
10 MINUTES   30 MINUTES

Middle-Eastern Style Chicken

SERVES 4	METRIC	IMPERIAL	AMERICAN
Oil	15 ml	1 tbsp	1 tbsp
Garlic cloves, 4 cut into slivers, 2 crushed	6	6	6
Large onion, sliced	1	1	1
Boneless chicken meat, thinly sliced	450 g	1 lb	1 lb
Celery stick, sliced	1	1	1
Large green (bell) pepper, cut into fine strips	1	1	1
Large courgette (zucchini), cubed	1	1	1
Lemon, finely sliced and each slice quartered	1	1	1
Can tomatoes	400 g	14 oz	1 large
Brown sugar	15 ml	1 tbsp	1 tbsp
Turmeric	10 ml	2 tsp	2 tsp
Chopped fresh oregano	30 ml	2 tbsp	2 tbsp
Thyme sprig	1	1	1
Salt and freshly ground black pepper			

1   Heat the wok or a large heavy-based frying pan.

2   Pour in the oil and when hot add the garlic, onion and chicken and stir-fry for 2–4 minutes until the chicken is tender.

3   Add the celery, pepper, courgette and lemon and cook for a further 3 minutes to tenderise the vegetables.

4 Roughly chop the tomatoes, then add to the pan with the remaining ingredients, seasoning to taste.

5 Stir well, cover and simmer for about 10 minutes.

SERVING SUGGESTION

Serve hot with boiled rice.

PREPARATION TIME: **COOKING TIME:**
15 MINUTES **20 MINUTES**

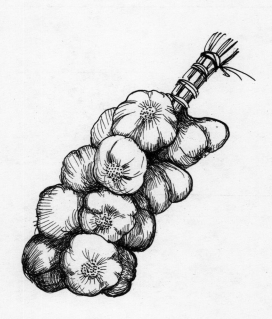

VERSATILE
VEGETABLES

★

Coconut Chick Peas

SERVES 4	METRIC	IMPERIAL	AMERICAN
Oil	15 ml	1 tbsp	1 tbsp
Garlic cloves, crushed	2	2	2
Onion, finely chopped	1	1	1
Mild green chillis, cut into fine strips	2	2	2
Cumin seeds	2.5 ml	½ tsp	½ tsp
Fenugreek seeds	2.5 ml	½ tsp	½ tsp
Salt	2.5 ml	½ tsp	½ tsp
Can chick peas (garbanzos), drained	440 g	15½ oz	1 large
Canned coconut milk	150 ml	¼ pt	⅔ cup
Chopped fresh coriander (cilantro)	15 ml	1 tbsp	1 tbsp

1 Heat the wok or a large heavy-based frying pan

2 Pour in the oil and when hot add the garlic, onion, chillis and spice seeds and stir-fry for about 1 minute.

3 Add the salt, chick peas and coconut milk. Reduce the heat slightly, cover and cook for 3–5 minutes.

4 Serve hot, sprinkled with the chopped coriander.

PREPARATION TIME: COOKING TIME:
10 MINUTES   8 MINUTES

Cheesy Nutty Parsnips

SERVES 4	METRIC	IMPERIAL	AMERICAN
Oil	30 ml	2 tbsp	2 tbsp
Par-boiled parsnips, cut into fine, short lengths	450 g	1 lb	1 lb
Cashew nuts	50 g	2 oz	½ cup
Parmesan cheese, very finely grated	30 ml	2 tbsp	2 tbsp
Celery salt	2.5 ml	½ tsp	½ tsp
Ground black pepper			

1   Heat the wok or a large heavy-based frying pan.

2   Pour in the oil and when hot add the parsnips and stir-fry for 2–3 minutes or until they are tender and slightly tinged brown.

3   Stir in the nuts and cook for a further minute.

4   Add the cheese, celery salt and pepper to taste. Stir well and serve hot.

PREPARATION TIME:
5 MINUTES

COOKING TIME:
6 MINUTES

Marrow with Ginger

SERVES 4	METRIC	IMPERIAL	AMERICAN
Oil	30 ml	2 tbsp	2 tbsp
Garlic clove, crushed	1	1	1
Chopped fresh root ginger	15 ml	1 tbsp	1 tbsp
Small shallot, finely chopped	1	1	1
Marrow, skinned, seeded and finely cubed	450 g	1 lb	1 lb
Balsamic vinegar	30 ml	2 tbsp	2 tbsp
Brown sugar	15 ml	1 tbsp	1 tbsp
Salt and freshly ground black pepper			

1 Heat the wok or a large heavy-based frying pan.

2 Pour in the oil and when hot stir-fry the garlic and ginger for a few seconds.

3 Add the shallot and cook for about 30 seconds.

4 Add the marrow and stir-fry for about 3–4 minutes or until tender.

5 Stir in the vinegar and sugar, then season to taste. Cook for a further minute, then serve.

PREPARATION TIME: 10 MINUTES COOKING TIME: 7 MINUTES

Crispy Greens

SERVES 4	METRIC	IMPERIAL	AMERICAN
Oil	60 ml	4 tbsp	4 tbsp
Spring greens (spring cabbage), very finely shredded	450 g	1 lb	1 lb
Salted peanuts, crushed	45 ml	3 tbsp	3 tbsp
Salt	5 ml	1 tsp	1 tsp

1 Heat the wok or a large heavy-based frying pan.

2 Pour in the oil and when very hot add the greens and stir-fry for about 3 minutes, turning frequently, until they are quite crisp.

3 Lift out with a draining spoon and place on a warm serving dish.

4 Mix the peanuts with the salt and sprinkle over the greens. Serve.

PREPARATION TIME:
5 MINUTES

COOKING TIME:
15 MINUTES

French Beans with Bacon

SERVES 4	METRIC	IMPERIAL	AMERICAN
Oil	15 ml	1 tbsp	1 tbsp
Small onion, finely chopped	1	1	1
Smoked bacon, finely chopped	50 g	2 oz	2 oz
French (green) beans, trimmed and cut into short lengths	450 g	1 lb	1 lb
Salt and freshly ground black pepper			

1   Heat the wok or a large heavy-based frying pan.

2   Pour in the oil and when hot add the onion and stir-fry for about 30 seconds.

3   Add the bacon and stir-fry for 2–3 minutes until slightly crisp.

4   Stir in the beans and cook until tender, probably 3 minutes or a little more.

5   Season to taste and serve.

PREPARATION TIME: 10 MINUTES   COOKING TIME: 8 MINUTES

Summer Salad Stir-fry

SERVES 4	METRIC	IMPERIAL	AMERICAN
Groundnut (peanut) oil	15 ml	1 tbsp	1 tbsp
Garlic clove, crushed	1	1	1
French (green) beans, cut into short lengths	100 g	4 oz	4 oz
Spring onions (scallions), finely chopped	5	5	5
Large celery stick, chopped	1	1	1
Courgette (zucchini), cut into short sticks	1	1	1
Chinese leaves, finely shredded	2	2	2
Honey	15 ml	1 tbsp	1 tbsp
Lemon juice	15 ml	1 tbsp	1 tbsp
Salt and freshly ground black pepper			
Sesame seeds	15 ml	1 tbsp	1 tbsp

1   Heat the wok or a large heavy-based frying pan.

2   Add the oil. When hot add the garlic, beans, onions, celery and courgette and stir-fry for a couple of minutes until the beans are slightly softened.

3   Stir in the Chinese leaves.

4   Add the honey, lemon juice, seasoning and sesame seeds.

5   Stir well and serve.

PREPARATION TIME: **COOKING TIME:**
10 MINUTES   **5 MINUTES**

'Grate' Veg

SERVES 4	METRIC	IMPERIAL	AMERICAN
Oil	30 ml	2 tbsp	2 tbsp
Potatoes, peeled and grated	175 g	6 oz	6 oz
Carrots, grated	100 g	4 oz	4 oz
Swede (rutabaga), grated	50 g	2 oz	2 oz
Onion, grated	1	1	1
Grated nutmeg	2.5 ml	½ tsp	½ tsp
Single (light) cream	60 ml	4 tbsp	4 tbsp
Salt and freshly ground black pepper			

1 Heat the wok or a large heavy-based frying pan.

2 Pour in the oil and when hot add all the grated vegetables and stir-fry for 3–5 minutes until they are quite soft, adding a little water if they start to stick to the pan.

3 Stir in the nutmeg and cream, then season to taste.

4 Heat through and serve.

PREPARATION TIME:
15 MINUTES

COOKING TIME:
8 MINUTES

Celery in Cheese Sauce

SERVES 4	METRIC	IMPERIAL	AMERICAN
Oil	15 ml	1 tbsp	1 tbsp
Shallots, finely chopped	2	2	2
Celery, finely sliced	450 g	1 lb	1 lb
Single (light) cream	150 ml	¼ pt	⅔ cup
Blue Brie, cubed	150 g	5 oz	1¼ cups
Salt and freshly ground black pepper			
Chopped fresh chives	15 ml	1 tbsp	1 tbsp

1   Heat the wok or a large heavy-based frying pan.

2   Pour in the oil and when hot add the shallots and celery and stir-fry for about 3 minutes or until the celery is quite tender.

3   Add the cream, then sprinkle in the cheese and stir until it is all melted.

4   Season to taste and serve with the chives scattered over the top.

PREPARATION TIME: COOKING TIME:
10 MINUTES · 5 MINUTES

Stir-fried Broccoli and Cauliflower

SERVES 4	METRIC	IMPERIAL	AMERICAN
Oil	30 ml	2 tbsp	2 tbsp
Garlic cloves, crushed	2	2	2
Chopped fresh root ginger	15 ml	1 tbsp	1 tbsp
Mild green chilli, finely chopped	1	1	1
Cauliflower florets, thinly sliced	225 g	8 oz	8 oz
Broccoli florets, thinly sliced	225 g	8 oz	8 oz
Soy sauce	15 ml	1 tbsp	1 tbsp
Dry sherry	15 ml	1 tbsp	1 tbsp
Pinch of sugar			
Salted peanuts, roughly crushed	25 g	1 oz	¼ cup

1 Heat the wok or a large heavy-based frying pan.

2 Pour in the oil and when hot add the garlic, ginger and chilli and cook for about 30 seconds.

3 Add the cauliflower and broccoli and stir-fry for 3–4 minutes so that both are slightly softened.

4 Stir in the soy sauce, sherry and sugar and heat the mixture through.

5 Serve hot with the peanuts scattered over the top.

PREPARATION TIME: **COOKING TIME:**
10 MINUTES   6 MINUTES

Lemon Carrots

SERVES 4	METRIC	IMPERIAL	AMERICAN
Oil	*15 ml*	*1 tbsp*	*1 tbsp*
Shallot, very finely chopped	*1*	*1*	*1*
Carrots, cut into thin, short sticks	*450 g*	*1 lb*	*1 lb*
Lemon juice	*45 ml*	*3 tbsp*	*3 tbsp*
Finely grated lemon zest	*15 ml*	*1 tbsp*	*1 tbsp*
Soft brown sugar	*15 ml*	*1 tbsp*	*1 tbsp*

1 Heat the wok or a large heavy-based frying pan.

2 Pour in the oil and when hot add the shallot and cook for 30 seconds.

3 Add the carrots and stir-fry for 3–4 minutes so that they are slightly softened.

4 Stir in the lemon juice, zest and sugar.

5 Heat through and serve as an accompaniment to a meal.

PREPARATION TIME: COOKING TIME:
5 MINUTES   6 MINUTES

Spinach with Almonds

SERVES 4	METRIC	IMPERIAL	AMERICAN
Oil	15 ml	1 tbsp	1 tbsp
Small onion, finely chopped	1	1	1
Garlic cloves, finely sliced	4	4	4
Spinach, hard stalks removed and roughly chopped	750 g	1½ lb	1½ lb
Soy sauce	15 ml	1 tbsp	1 tbsp
Pinch of sugar			
Flaked almonds	50 g	2 oz	½ cup
Pinch of freshly ground black pepper			

1 Heat the wok or a large heavy-based frying pan.

2 Pour in the oil and when hot stir-fry the onion and garlic for 30–60 seconds until browned slightly.

3 Add the spinach and stir for about 2 minutes until it is wilted.

4 Stir in the remaining ingredients and cook for a further 2 minutes.

5 Serve hot.

PREPARATION TIME:
10 MINUTES

COOKING TIME:
5 MINUTES

Curried Vegetables

SERVES 4	METRIC	IMPERIAL	AMERICAN
Large carrots, thickly sliced	3	3	3
Large courgettes (zucchini), thickly sliced	2	2	2
Celery sticks, cut into short lengths	2	2	2
Oil	30 ml	2 tbsp	2 tbsp
Garlic cloves, crushed	2	2	2
Chopped fresh root ginger	15 ml	1 tbsp	1 tbsp
Large onion, sliced	1	1	1
Small red (bell) pepper, sliced	1	1	1
Button mushrooms	50 g	2 oz	2 oz
Medium-hot curry paste, from a jar or can	45 ml	3 tbsp	3 tbsp
Canned coconut milk	150 ml	¼ pt	⅔ cup
Water	150 ml	¼ pt	⅔ cup
Chopped fresh coriander (cilantro)	15 ml	1 tbsp	1 tbsp

1 Bring a saucepan of water to the boil, then immerse the carrots and cook for a couple of minutes.

2 Add the courgettes and celery and cook for a further minute. Drain well.

3 Heat the wok or a large heavy-based frying pan.

4 Pour in the oil and when hot stir-fry the garlic and ginger for a few seconds.

5 Add the onion and pepper and stir-fry for 1 minute.

6 Add the par-boiled vegetables to the pan with the mushrooms and cook, stirring, for about 3 minutes or until all the vegetables are quite tender.

7 Stir in the curry paste followed by the coconut milk and water and cook for a further 3 minutes so that all the ingredients are hot and the sauce slightly thickened.

8 Serve garnished with the chopped coriander.

PREPARATION TIME:
15 MINUTES

COOKING TIME:
15 MINUTES

Tofu with Mediterranean Vegetables

SERVES 4	METRIC	IMPERIAL	AMERICAN
Aubergine (eggplant), cubed	1	1	1
Salt and white pepper			
Tofu, drained and cut into 1 cm/½ in cubes	2 × 285 g packs	2 × 10½ oz packs	2 × 10½ oz packs
Oil	30 ml	2 tbsp	2 tbsp
Garlic cloves, crushed	2	2	2
Large onion, sliced	1	1	1
Small red (bell) pepper, thinly sliced	1	1	1
Small green (bell) pepper, thinly sliced	1	1	1
Courgette (zucchini), sliced	1	1	1
Large tomatoes, skinned and chopped	3	3	3
Torn basil leaves	30 ml	2 tbsp	2 tbsp
Tomato purée (paste)	30 ml	2 tbsp	2 tbsp
Mozzarella cheese, cut into small cubes	50 g	2 oz	½ cup

1   Place the cubed aubergine on a plate and sprinkle with salt. Leave for 20 minutes, then rinse under cold running water.

2   Coat the cubed tofu with salt and pepper.

3   Heat the wok or a large heavy-based frying pan.

4   Pour in the oil and when hot add the tofu and stir-fry for

approximately 4 minutes or until it is browned all over.

5 Add the garlic, onion, peppers and aubergine to the pan and continue to stir-fry for about 4 minutes until the vegetables are softened.

6 Stir in the courgette and tomatoes and cook for 1–2 minutes.

7 Add the basil leaves and tomato purée. Season to taste and heat through.

8 Spoon into individual heatproof bowls and sprinkle the cubed Mozzarella over the top.

9 Place under a very hot grill (broiler) for a few minutes to melt and slightly brown the cheese.

PREPARATION TIME:
15 MINUTES PLUS
20 MINUTES TO SALT
THE AUBERGINES

COOKING TIME:
15 MINUTES

Chicory with Pears

SERVES 4	METRIC	IMPERIAL	AMERICAN
Oil	*15 ml*	*1 tbsp*	*1 tbsp*
Small red onion, *finely chopped*	*1*	*1*	*1*

Chicory (Belgian endive)
    heads, finely sliced
    crosswise
	3	*3*	*3*

Firm pears, peeled, *cored and diced*	*3*	*3*	*3*
Balsamic vinegar	*30 ml*	*2 tbsp*	*2 tbsp*
Pinch of sugar			
Pinch of ground cloves			
Salt and freshly ground black pepper			

1   Heat the wok or a large heavy-based frying pan.

2   Heat the oil, then stir-fry the onion for about 1 minute.

3   Add the chicory and pears and stir-fry for 2 minutes or until the chicory is just slightly softened.

4   Stir in the vinegar, sugar and cloves, then season to taste.

5   Heat through and serve.

PREPARATION TIME: COOKING TIME:
10 MINUTES   5 MINUTES

Sugared Green Tomatoes

SERVES 4	METRIC	IMPERIAL	AMERICAN
Oil	*15 ml*	*1 tbsp*	*1 tbsp*
Green tomatoes, thinly sliced	*450 g*	*1 lb*	*1 lb*
Demerara sugar	*30 ml*	*2 tbsp*	*2 tbsp*

1   Heat the wok or a large heavy-based frying pan.

2   Add the oil and when hot add the tomatoes and stir-fry for about 3 minutes or until they are softened but still retain some shape.

3   Carefully stir in the brown sugar and serve hot.

PREPARATION TIME:
3 MINUTES

COOKING TIME:
4 MINUTES

Simple Vegetable Stir-fry

SERVES 4	METRIC	IMPERIAL	AMERICAN
Oil	15 ml	1 tbsp	1 tbsp
Garlic cloves, crushed	2	2	2
Chopped fresh root ginger	15 ml	1 tbsp	1 tbsp
Spring onions (scallions), chopped	4	4	4
Mangetout (snow peas), trimmed	225 g	8 oz	8 oz
Baby sweetcorn (corn), fresh or thawed frozen	12	12	12
Button mushrooms, quartered	100 g	4 oz	4 oz
Soy sauce	15 ml	1 tbsp	1 tbsp
Oyster sauce	15 ml	1 tbsp	1 tbsp
Pinch of sugar			

1   Heat the wok or a large heavy-based frying pan.

2   Pour in the oil and when hot add the garlic and ginger and cook for a few seconds.

3   Add the spring onions, mangetout, sweetcorn and mushrooms and stir-fry for about 2 minutes so that they are all slightly softened.

4   Stir in the remaining ingredients and cook for a further minute, then serve.

PREPARATION TIME: **COOKING TIME:**
10 MINUTES   4 MINUTES

Christmas Sprouts

SERVES 4	METRIC	IMPERIAL	AMERICAN
Oil	15 ml	1 tbsp	1 tbsp
Small shallot, chopped	1	1	1
Brussels sprouts, par-boiled and halved	450 g	1 lb	1 lb
Whole tinned chestnuts, shelled and drained	100 g	4 oz	4 oz
Pinch of ground cinnamon			
Port	15 ml	1 tbsp	1 tbsp
Salt and freshly ground black pepper			

1 Heat the wok or a large heavy-based frying pan.

2 Pour in the oil and when hot add the shallot and stir-fry for about 1 minute or until it is soft.

3 Add the Brussels sprouts to the pan and cook for 2–3 minutes.

4 Stir in the chestnuts, cinnamon and port and season to taste.

5 Cook for another minute or so to heat through, then serve.

PREPARATION TIME:
5 MINUTES
COOKING TIME:
7 MINUTES

Herby Leeks

SERVES 4	METRIC	IMPERIAL	AMERICAN
Oil	15 ml	1 tbsp	1 tbsp
Leeks, finely sliced	3	3	3
Green (bell) pepper, diced	1	1	1
Chopped fresh thyme	10 ml	2 tsp	2 tsp
Chopped fresh parsley	15 ml	1 tbsp	1 tbsp
Chopped fresh sage	5 ml	1 tsp	1 tsp
Chopped fresh rosemary	5 ml	1 tsp	1 tsp
Vegetable stock	60 ml	4 tbsp	4 tbsp
Salt and freshly ground black pepper			

1 Heat the wok or a large heavy-based frying pan.

2 Pour in the oil and when hot add the leeks and diced pepper and stir-fry for about 4 minutes.

3 Stir in the fresh herbs and cook for 1 minute.

4 Add the stock and season to taste.

5 Heat through and serve.

PREPARATION TIME: COOKING TIME:
15 MINUTES   9 MINUTES

Chutney-style Vegetables

SERVES 4	METRIC	IMPERIAL	AMERICAN
Oil	30 ml	2 tbsp	2 tbsp
Garlic clove, crushed	1	1	1
Chopped fresh root ginger	10 ml	2 tsp	2 tsp
Small red chilli, finely chopped	1	1	1
Onion, chopped	1	1	1
Marrow, peeled, seeded and finely cubed	225 g	8 oz	8 oz
Eating (dessert) apples, peeled, cored and finely cubed	2	2	2
Red (bell) pepper, diced	1	1	1
Brown sugar	30 ml	2 tbsp	2 tbsp
White wine vinegar	30 ml	2 tbsp	2 tbsp
Pinch of ground allspice			
Salt and freshly ground black pepper			

1 Heat the wok or a large heavy-based frying pan.

2 Pour in the oil and when hot add the garlic, ginger and chilli and cook for 30 seconds.

3 Place the onion in the pan and stir-fry for another minute.

4 Add the marrow, apple and red pepper and cook, stirring, for 4–5 minutes or until all the vegetables are quite soft.

5 Stir in the remaining ingredients, season to taste and cook for a further 2–3 minutes.

SERVING SUGGESTION

Serve hot with cold meats.

PREPARATION TIME: 15 MINUTES COOKING TIME: 12 MINUTES

Stir-fried Cucumber

SERVES 4	METRIC	IMPERIAL	AMERICAN
Cucumbers, peeled, seeded and cut into short sticks	1½	1½	1½
Salt			
Oil	15 ml	1 tbsp	1 tbsp
Garlic clove, crushed	1	1	1
Chopped fresh ginger	5 ml	1 tsp	1 tsp
Black bean sauce	15 ml	1 tbsp	1 tbsp
Pinch of five-spice powder			
Soy sauce	10 ml	2 tsp	2 tsp
Dry sherry	5 ml	1 tsp	1 tsp
Pinch of sugar			

1   Place the cucumber on a plate and sprinkle with salt. Leave for 20 minutes to remove any excess liquid, then rinse in cold water and pat dry with kitchen paper.

2   Heat the wok or a large heavy-based frying pan.

3   Pour in the oil and when hot add the garlic and ginger and cook for a few seconds.

4   Add the cucumber to the pan and stir-fry for a further few seconds.

5   Stir in all the remaining ingredients and cook for 3 minutes.

6   Serve hot.

PREPARATION TIME:
10 MINUTES PLUS
20 MINUTES TO SALT
THE CUCUMBER

COOKING TIME:
5 MINUTES

Tofu with Mushrooms

SERVES 4	METRIC	IMPERIAL	AMERICAN
Small red chilli, finely chopped	*1*	*1*	*1*
Soy sauce	*15 ml*	*1 tbsp*	*1 tbsp*
Vinegar	*15 ml*	*1 tbsp*	*1 tbsp*
Pinch of five-spice powder			
Garlic cloves, crushed	*3*	*3*	*3*
Tofu, drained and thinly sliced	*285 g pack*	*10½ oz pack*	*10½ oz pack*
Oil	*15 ml*	*1 tbsp*	*1 tbsp*
Large onion, finely sliced	*1*	*1*	*1*
Button mushrooms, quartered	*225 g*	*8 oz*	*8 oz*

1   Combine the chilli, soy sauce, vinegar, spice and garlic and use to marinate the tofu for about 10 minutes.

2   Heat the wok or a large heavy-based frying pan.

3   Pour in the oil and when hot fry the onion for 1 minute.

4   Reserving the marinade, add the tofu to the pan and stir-fry for about 5 minutes or until quite brown all over.

5   Add the mushrooms to the pan and cook for 1 minute.

6   Stir in the reserved marinade and cook for 2–3 minutes.

7   Serve hot.

PREPARATION TIME:
5 MINUTES PLUS
10 MINUTES
MARINATING TIME

COOKING TIME:
10 MINUTES

Crunchy Noodles

SERVES 4	METRIC	IMPERIAL	AMERICAN
Oil	30 ml	2 tbsp	2 tbsp
Spring onions (scallions), roughly chopped	4	4	4
Mangetout (snow peas), trimmed	50 g	2 oz	2 oz
Baby sweetcorn (corn), fresh or thawed frozen	12	12	12
Radishes, sliced	25 g	1 oz	1 oz
Precooked medium egg noodles, drained	175 g	6 oz	6 oz
Chilli oil	5 ml	1 tsp	1 tsp
Soy sauce	10 ml	2 tsp	2 tsp

❋

1 Heat the wok or a large heavy-based frying pan.

2 Pour in the 30 ml/2 tbsp oil and when hot add all the vegetables and stir-fry for about 2 minutes or until they are slightly softened.

3 Remove the vegetables from the pan with a draining spoon and keep warm.

4 Reheat the pan ensuring that there is at least 15 ml/1 tbsp oil left in it.

5 Place the noodles in the pan and stir infrequently for about 4–5 minutes or until they have formed a crispy crust.

6 Serve the noodles with the vegetables on top and then drizzle the chilli oil and soy sauce all over.

PREPARATION TIME: COOKING TIME:
10 MINUTES   9 MINUTES

SIMPLY SNACKS

★

Supreme Scrambled Eggs

SERVES 4	METRIC	IMPERIAL	AMERICAN
Oil	15 ml	1 tbsp	1 tbsp
Spring onions (scallions), finely chopped	4	4	4
Small red (bell) pepper, diced	1	1	1
Smoked bacon, finely chopped	100 g	4 oz	4 oz
Eggs	4	4	4
Single (light) cream	120 ml	4 fl oz	½ cup
Salt and freshly ground black pepper			
Cheddar cheese, grated	50 g	2 oz	½ cup

1 Heat the wok or a large heavy-based frying pan.

2 Add the oil and heat, then stir in the spring onions, pepper and bacon and stir-fry for about 1 minute or until the bacon is cooked.

3 Beat the eggs quickly with the cream, salt and pepper, then pour into the pan.

4 Stir the egg mixture until it starts to scramble, then add the cheese.

5 Cook, stirring, until all the egg has scrambled.

SERVING SUGGESTION

Serve with buttered toast.

PREPARATION TIME:
10 MINUTES

COOKING TIME:
5 MINUTES

Creamed Corn Brunch

SERVES 4	METRIC	IMPERIAL	AMERICAN
Oil	30 ml	2 tbsp	2 tbsp
Small onion, finely chopped	1	1	1
Herby sausages, cut into bite-sized pieces	450 g	1 lb	1 lb
Can creamed sweetcorn (corn)	300 g	11 oz	1 large
Thick slices wholemeal bread, toasted	4	4	4

1   Heat the wok or a large heavy-based frying pan.

2   Pour in the oil and when hot stir-fry the onion for 1 minute.

3   Add the sausages and stir-fry for about 4 minutes or until browned and cooked on the inside.

4   Drain any excess oil from the pan, then add the creamed sweetcorn.

5   Season to taste, then stir and heat the mixture through.

6   Divide the mixture between the slices of toast and serve.

PREPARATION TIME: COOKING TIME:
5 MINUTES   7 MINUTES

Nut Nibbles

SERVES 4	METRIC	IMPERIAL	AMERICAN
Oil	60 ml	4 tbsp	4 tbsp
Blanched almonds	100 g	4 oz	1 cup
Large shelled peanuts	100 g	4 oz	1 cup
Cashew nuts	100 g	4 oz	1 cup
Walnut halves	100 g	4 oz	1 cup
Soft brown sugar	30 ml	2 tbsp	2 tbsp
Grated nutmeg	2.5 ml	½ tsp	½ tsp
Ground cinnamon	10 ml	2 tsp	2 tsp

1. Heat the wok or a large heavy-based frying pan.

2. Add the oil and when very hot add all the nuts and stir-fry until they are browned, probably about 2–3 minutes.

3. Drain off any excess oil, then return to the heat and stir in the sugar and spices.

SERVING SUGGESTION

Serve warm or cold as a dish of nibbles to go with drinks. Can be stored in a screw-top jar.

PREPARATION TIME: NONE COOKING TIME: 4 MINUTES

Five-minute Fried Rice

SERVES 4	METRIC	IMPERIAL	AMERICAN
Oil	30 ml	2 tbsp	2 tbsp
Cold precooked long-grain rice	450 g	1 lb	2 cups
Smoked ham, diced	100 g	4 oz	½ cup
Curry powder	5 ml	1 tsp	1 tsp
Salt	5 ml	1 tsp	1 tsp
Eggs, beaten	2	2	2
Spring onions (scallions), finely chopped	3	3	3
Salted peanuts	25 g	1 oz	¼ cup

1 Heat the wok or a large heavy-based frying pan.

2 Pour in the oil and when hot add the rice and stir-fry for about 2 minutes.

3 Add the ham to the pan and cook for 30 seconds.

4 Stir in the curry powder and salt, then the beaten eggs and stir for about 2 minutes or until the egg is set.

5 Serve hot with the spring onion and peanuts sprinkled over.

PREPARATION TIME: COOKING TIME:
5 MINUTES   15 MINUTES

Creamy Mushrooms and Prawns

SERVES 4	METRIC	IMPERIAL	AMERICAN
Oil	15 ml	1 tbsp	1 tbsp
Garlic clove, crushed	1	1	1
Shallot, finely chopped	1	1	1
Button mushrooms, quartered	225 g	8 oz	8 oz
Cooked prawns (shrimp)	225 g	8 oz	1 cup
Paprika	2.5 ml	½ tsp	½ tsp
Soured (dairy sour) cream	150 ml	¼ pt	⅔ cup
Salt and freshly ground black pepper			

1 Heat the wok or a large heavy-based frying pan.

2 Pour in the oil and when hot stir-fry the garlic and shallot for 30 seconds.

3 Add the mushrooms and cook for about 2 minutes.

4 Stir in the prawns and the remaining ingredients.

5 Heat through and serve.

PREPARATION TIME:
5 MINUTES

COOKING TIME:
4 MINUTES

Mini Mediterranean-style Munchies

SERVES 4	METRIC	IMPERIAL	AMERICAN
Medium French stick	1	1	1
Oil	15 ml	1 tbsp	1 tbsp
Garlic cloves, crushed	2	2	2
Spanish onion, finely sliced	1	1	1
Large red (bell) pepper, cut into fine rings	1	1	1
Large yellow or orane (bell) pepper, cut into fine rings	1	1	1
Tomato purée (paste)	30 ml	2 tbsp	2 tbsp
Can anchovies, drained	100 g	4 oz	1 small
Black olives, stoned (pitted)	12	12	12
Chopped fresh oregano or marjoram	15 ml	1 tbsp	1 tbsp
Salt and freshly ground black pepper			

1   Slice the French stick in half lengthways, then cut each half into two.

2   Heat the wok or a large heavy-based frying pan.

3   Pour in the oil and when hot add the garlic and stir-fry for a few seconds.

4   Add the onion and peppers and stir-fry for 2 minutes until soft.

5   Add the tomato purée, anchovies, olives and herbs and heat through, stirring, for about 1 minute.

6   Season, then pile the mixture on the bread and serve.

PREPARATION TIME: **COOKING TIME:**
10 MINUTES   5 MINUTES

Monday Fry

SERVES 4	METRIC	IMPERIAL	AMERICAN
Oil	*15 ml*	*1 tbsp*	*1 tbsp*
Onion, sliced	*1*	*1*	*1*
Cold roast potatoes, diced	*225 g*	*8 oz*	*2 cups*
Cold cooked white cabbage or cold cooked Brussels sprouts, sliced	*225 g*	*8 oz*	*2 cups*
Cold gravy	*30 ml*	*2 tbsp*	*2 tbsp*

Salt and freshly ground black pepper

1 Heat the wok or a large heavy-based frying pan.

2 Pour in the oil and when hot fry the onion for 1–2 minutes or until softened.

3 Add the potato and cabbage or sprouts to the pan and stir-fry for 1 minute.

4 Stir in the gravy to moisten the mixture and heat through.

5 Season to taste and serve piping hot.

**PREPARATION TIME:
5 MINUTES**

**COOKING TIME:
5 MINUTES**

Salmon Noodle Snack

SERVES 4	METRIC	IMPERIAL	AMERICAN
Oil	15 ml	1 tbsp	1 tbsp
Garlic clove, crushed	1	1	1
Spring onions (scallions), finely chopped	4	4	4
Mangetout (snow peas)	50 g	2 oz	2 oz
Precooked medium egg noodles, drained	350 g	12 oz	12 oz
Can pink salmon, drained	215 g	7½ oz	1 med
Lemon juice	15 ml	1 tbsp	1 tbsp
Chopped fresh parsley	15 ml	1 tbsp	1 tbsp
Salt and freshly ground black pepper			

1   Heat the wok or a large heavy-based frying pan.

2   Pour in the oil and when hot add the garlic and spring onions and stir-fry for 30 seconds.

3   Add the mangetout and cook for a further minute.

4   Stir in all the remaining ingredients, ensuring that they are well combined, heat through and serve.

PREPARATION TIME:
5 MINUTES

COOKING TIME:
5 MINUTES

Summer Tomatoes and Beans

SERVES 4	METRIC	IMPERIAL	AMERICAN
Oil	15 ml	1 tbsp	1 tbsp
Spring onions (scallions), sliced	3	3	3
Large ripe tomatoes, skinned, seeded and sliced	450 g	1 lb	1 lb
Can flageolet beans, drained	300 g	11 oz	1 large
Shredded fresh sweet basil leaves	30 ml	2 tbsp	2 tbsp
Lemon juice	15 ml	1 tbsp	1 tbsp
Sugar	5 ml	1 tsp	1 tsp
Extra virgin olive oil	5 ml	1 tsp	1 tsp
Salt and freshly ground black pepper			

1 Heat the wok or a large heavy-based frying pan.

2 Pour in the oil and when hot add the spring onions and tomatoes and cook for 1–2 minutes so that the tomatoes are starting to soften but still retain a little shape.

3 Stir in the beans and basil leaves and cook for a further 30 seconds.

4 Add the remaining ingredients, seasoning to taste, and serve hot or cold.

PREPARATION TIME: COOKING TIME:
10 MINUTES   4 MINUTES

Breakfast-style Stir-fry

SERVES 4	METRIC	IMPERIAL	AMERICAN
Oil	*15 ml*	*1 tbsp*	*1 tbsp*
Thick smoked bacon, diced	*350 g*	*12 oz*	*12 oz*
Button mushrooms, quartered	*175 g*	*6 oz*	*6 oz*
Cherry tomatoes	*100 g*	*4 oz*	*4 oz*
Worcestershire sauce	*10 ml*	*2 tsp*	*2 tsp*
Salt and freshly ground black pepper			

1   Heat the wok or a large heavy-based frying pan.

2   Pour in the oil and heat, then add the bacon and fry (sauté) for 2–3 minutes or until it has changed colour.

3   Add the mushrooms and stir-fry for a further minute.

4   Stir in the tomatoes and Worcestershire sauce and cook for a further minute, then season to taste.

SERVING SUGGESTION

Serve with buttered toast.

PREPARATION TIME:
5 MINUTES

COOKING TIME:
7 MINUTES

Spicy Lamb Pockets

SERVES 4	METRIC	IMPERIAL	AMERICAN
Plain (all-purpose) flour	15 ml	1 tbsp	1 tbsp
Curry powder	5 ml	1 tsp	1 tsp
Ground cumin	2.5 ml	½ tsp	½ tsp
Pinch of ground cinnamon			
Pinch of chilli powder			
Salt and freshly ground black pepper			
Boneless lamb, cut into fine strips	350 g	12 oz	12 oz
Oil	30 ml	2 tbsp	2 tbsp
Lemon juice	15 ml	1 tbsp	1 tbsp
Large pitta breads	4	4	4
Mango chutney	60 ml	4 tbsp	4 tbsp
Crisp lettuce leaves, finely shredded	4	4	4
Small onion, finely sliced	1	1	1

1   Combine the flour with the spices and salt and pepper and use to coat the lamb.

2   Heat the wok or a large heavy-based frying pan.

3   Pour in the oil and when very hot add the lamb and stir-fry for about 4 minutes or until it is tender and slightly crisp on the outside, then stir in the lemon juice.

4   Lift the lamb out of the pan with a draining spoon and keep warm.

5 Split the pitta breads and spread 15 ml/1 tbsp of the chutney in each.

6 Divide the shredded lettuce, onion and lamb between the pitta breads and serve hot.

PREPARATION TIME: COOKING TIME:
10 MINUTES   6 MINUTES

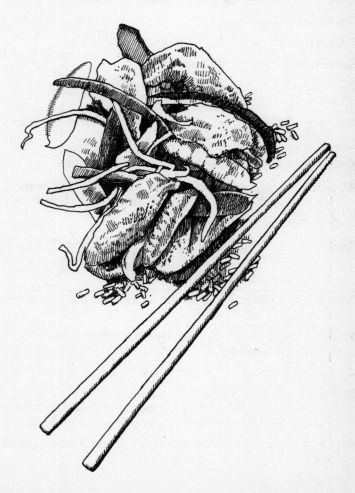

Spicy Chick Peas

SERVES 4	METRIC	IMPERIAL	AMERICAN
Dried chick peas (garbanzos)	175 g	6 oz	¾ cup
Oil	90 ml	6 tbsp	6 tbsp
Salt	5 ml	1 tsp	1 tsp
Chilli powder	5 ml	1 tsp	1 tsp
Pinch of sugar			
Pinch of cumin			

1   Soak the chick peas in cold water for at least 4 hours, preferably overnight, then drain.

2   Heat the wok or a large heavy-based frying pan.

3   Pour in the oil and when very hot add the chick peas and stir-fry for about 2–3 minutes until they are crisp and slightly browned.

4   Lift out with a draining spoon and while they are still very hot, mix in the salt, spices and sugar.

SERVING SUGGESTION

Serve cold as a side dish or as nibbles with drinks.

PREPARATION TIME:
4 HOURS SOAKING
(MINIMUM)

COOKING TIME:
4 MINUTES

Caraway Cauliflower with Ham and Cheese

SERVES 4	METRIC	IMPERIAL	AMERICAN
Cauliflower	350 g	12 oz	12 oz
Oil	30 ml	2 tbsp	2 tbsp
Small onion, finely chopped	1	1	1
Caraway seeds	15 ml	1 tbsp	1 tbsp
Sliced ham, cut into fine strips	100 g	4 oz	½ cup
Cream cheese	100 g	4 oz	½ cup
Salt and freshly ground black pepper			

1   Cut the cauliflower into very small florets and shred any thick stems.

2   Heat the wok or a large heavy-based frying pan.

3   Pour in the oil and when hot add the cauliflower and onion and stir-fry for about 4 minutes or until both are quite tender.

4   Add the caraway seeds and ham and cook for 30 seconds.

5   Stir in the cream cheese and cook until it has melted, then season to taste, mix well and serve hot.

PREPARATION TIME: COOKING TIME:
10 MINUTES   7 MINUTES

Curried Eggs with Smoked Haddock

SERVES 4	METRIC	IMPERIAL	AMERICAN
Oil	15 ml	1 tbsp	1 tbsp
Small onion, finely chopped	1	1	1
Mild curry powder	5 ml	1 tsp	1 tsp
Pinch of turmeric			
Pinch of cumin			
Large tomatoes, skinned and chopped	2	2	2
Single (light) cream	30 ml	2 tbsp	2 tbsp
Natural yoghurt	30 ml	2 tbsp	2 tbsp
Smoked haddock, cut into thick strips	350 g	12 oz	12 oz
Hard-boiled (hard-cooked) eggs, quartered	4	4	4
Salt and freshly ground black pepper			
Chopped fresh coriander (cilantro)	5 ml	1 tsp	1 tsp

1   Heat the wok or a large heavy-based frying pan.

2   Pour in the oil and when hot add the onion and cook for 2–3 minutes or until soft.

3   Stir in the spices and cook for 30 seconds.

4   Add the tomatoes, cream and yoghurt and cook, stirring, for about 2 minutes until heated through.

5 Finally, gently stir in the fish and eggs and cook for 2–3 minutes only, to ensure that the fish is done. Season to taste.

6 Serve with the coriander sprinkled over the top.

PREPARATION TIME: COOKING TIME:
10 MINUTES   10 MINUTES

Prawn and Potato Lunch

SERVES 4	METRIC	IMPERIAL	AMERICAN
Oil	30 ml	2 tbsp	2 tbsp
Small red onion, chopped	1	1	1
Par-boiled potato, diced	225 g	8 oz	8 oz
Cooked prawns (shrimp)	225 g	8 oz	½ cup
Chopped fresh parsley	15 ml	1 tbsp	1 tbsp
Salt and freshly ground black pepper			
Eggs, beaten	4	4	4

1 Heat the wok or a large heavy-based frying pan.

2 Pour in the oil and when hot add the onion and cook for about a minute.

3 Add the potato to the pan and stir-fry for a further minute, then stir in the prawns and parsley and cook for a few seconds.

4 Season to taste, then pour over the beaten eggs and reduce the heat very slightly. Do not agitate the eggs but allow to set for a few minutes to form a thick omelette.

5 Turn the omelette over and allow to set.

6 Cut into thick chunks and serve hot or cold.

PREPARATION TIME:
5 MINUTES

COOKING TIME:
10 MINUTES

Ham and Courgette Supper

SERVES 4	METRIC	IMPERIAL	AMERICAN
Oil	15 ml	1 tbsp	1 tbsp
Shallot, finely chopped	1	1	1
Courgettes (zucchini), cut into fine, short sticks	2	2	2
Thick ham, finely cubed	350 g	12 oz	1½ cups
Feta cheese, crumbled	100 g	4 oz	1 cup

1   Heat the wok or a large heavy-based frying pan.

2   Pour in the oil and when hot add the shallot and cook for 30 seconds.

3   Add the courgettes to the pan and stir-fry for about 3 minutes or until they soften slightly.

4   Stir in the ham and cook briefly to heat through.

5   Spoon the mixture into individual bowls and sprinkle the feta cheese on top while still very hot.

PREPARATION TIME: **COOKING TIME:**
10 MINUTES **6 MINUTES**

DELECTABLE
DESSERTS

★

Chocolate Melt

SERVES 4	METRIC	IMPERIAL	AMERICAN
Oil	15 ml	1 tbsp	1 tbsp
Chocolate sponge cake, cut in small cubes	225 g	8 oz	8 oz
Pecan nuts, halved	50 g	2 oz	½ cup
Plain (semi-sweet) chocolate, grated	50 g	2 oz	½ cup
Marshmallows	50 g	2 oz	2 oz
Crème fraîche	60 ml	4 tbsp	4 tbsp

1   Heat the wok or a large heavy-based frying pan.

2   Pour in the oil and when hot add the cake and stir-fry for 1–2 minutes until slightly crisp on the edges.

3   Add the nuts and cook for a further minute.

4   Stir in the grated chocolate and marshmallows and cook until all the chocolate has melted and the marshmallows are just starting to melt.

5   Pile into four individual serving dishes and top each with 15 ml/1 tbsp of crème fraîche.

PREPARATION TIME:
5 MINUTES

COOKING TIME:
5 MINUTES

Hot Orange with Chestnuts

SERVES 4	METRIC	IMPERIAL	AMERICAN
Oil	15 ml	1 tbsp	1 tbsp
Canned shelled chestnuts, sliced	100 g	4 oz	4 oz
Large oranges, peeled, segmented and membrane removed	3	3	3
Icing (confectioners') sugar	15 ml	1 tbsp	1 tbsp
Fresh orange juice	30 ml	2 tbsp	2 tbsp
Cointreau	15 ml	1 tbsp	1 tbsp

1 Heat the wok or a large heavy-based frying pan.

2 Pour in the oil and when hot add the chestnut slices and stir-fry for about 2 minutes or until they are slightly browned.

3 Add the orange segments and cook for 1 minute.

4 Stir in the sugar, juice and Cointreau, heat the mixture through and serve hot.

PREPARATION TIME: COOKING TIME:
15 MINUTES   5 MINUTES

Melba Cubes with Cherries

SERVES 4	METRIC	IMPERIAL	AMERICAN
Thick white bread slices	3	3	3
Egg, beaten	1	1	1
Icing (confectioners') sugar	15 ml	1 tbsp	1 tbsp
Ground cinnamon	7.5 ml	1½ tsp	1½ tsp
Oil	30 ml	2 tbsp	2 tbsp
Can stoned (pitted) cherries, drained and syrup reserved	410 g	14½ oz	1 large
Sugar	10 ml	2 tsp	2 tsp

1   Remove and discard the crusts from the bread and cut into 2.5 cm/1 in cubes.

2   Combine the egg, icing sugar and cinnamon and pour over the bread cubes. Mix well and leave to soak for 10 minutes.

3   Heat the wok or a large heavy-based frying pan.

4   Pour in the oil and when hot add the bread cubes and stir-fry for 1–2 minutes until brown and crisp all over.

5   Stir in the cherries, 30 ml/2 tbsp of the reserved syrup and the sugar and heat through for a few seconds.

SERVING SUGGESTION

Serve hot with chilled cream or yoghurt.

PREPARATION TIME:
3 MINUTES PLUS 10
MINUTES TO SOAK
THE BREAD

COOKING TIME:
4 MINUTES

Honeyed Exotic Fruits

SERVES 4	METRIC	IMPERIAL	AMERICAN
Medium pineapple	½	½	½
Oil	15 ml	1 tbsp	1 tbsp
Sesame seeds	30 ml	2 tbsp	2 tbsp
Mango, peeled, stoned (pitted) and cubed	1	1	1
Nectarine, stoned (pitted) and sliced	1	1	1
Seedless grapes	50 g	2 oz	⅓ cup
Kiwi fruits, peeled and thickly sliced	2	2	2
Clear honey	45 ml	3 tbsp	3 tbsp

1 Skin and core the pineapple and cut the flesh into 2.5 cm/1 in cubes.

2 Heat the wok or a large heavy-based frying pan.

3 Pour in the oil and when hot add the sesame seeds and cook for a few seconds.

4 Add all the fruit and stir-fry for about 3 minutes.

5 Stir in the honey, heat through and serve hot.

PREPARATION TIME:
20 MINUTES

COOKING TIME:
5 MINUTES

Peaches with Sweet White Wine

SERVES 4	METRIC	IMPERIAL	AMERICAN
Oil	15 ml	1 tbsp	1 tbsp
Fresh peaches, skinned, stoned (pitted) and sliced	4	4	4
Sweet white wine	90 ml	6 tbsp	6 tbsp
Ground almonds	30 ml	2 tbsp	2 tbsp
Icing (confectioners') sugar	15 ml	1 tbsp	1 tbsp
Flaked almonds, lightly toasted	30 ml	2 tbsp	2 tbsp

1   Heat the wok or a large heavy-based frying pan.

2   Pour in the oil and when hot add the peach slices and gently stir-fry for about 5 minutes or until they are tinged brown.

3   Add the wine and cook for a minute or so to reduce the amount of liquid slightly.

4   Stir in the ground almonds and icing sugar and cook for a further minute.

5   Serve hot, topped with the flaked almonds.

PREPARATION TIME: 5 MINUTES   COOKING TIME: 9 MINUTES

Madeira Bananas
with Butterscotch Sauce

SERVES 4	METRIC	IMPERIAL	AMERICAN
Oil	15 ml	1 tbsp	1 tbsp
Madeira cake, cut into small cubes	100 g	4 oz	4 oz
Small bananas, sliced	4	4	4
Walnut pieces	50 g	2 oz	½ cup
For the sauce:			
Soft brown sugar	30 ml	2 tbsp	2 tbsp
Granulated sugar	30 ml	2 tbsp	2 tbsp
Butter	30 ml	2 tbsp	2 tbsp
Golden (light corn) syrup	15 ml	1 tbsp	1 tbsp
Double (heavy) cream	75 ml	5 tbsp	5 tbsp

1 Heat the wok or a large heavy-based frying pan.

2 Pour in the oil and heat, then add the cake, bananas and walnuts and stir fry for 1–2 minutes or until the cake is slightly tinged brown on the edges.

3 Remove the banana mixture from the pan and keep warm.

4 To make the sauce, place all the ingredients except the cream in the wok and stir until they have completely melted and combined.

5 Stir in the cream and heat through.

6 Serve the banana mixture in individual bowls with the sauce drizzled over.

PREPARATION TIME: **COOKING TIME:**
5 MINUTES   6 MINUTES

Recycled Pancakes

SERVES 4	METRIC	IMPERIAL	AMERICAN
Oil	30 ml	2 tbsp	2 tbsp
Leftover or ready-made pancakes, cut into thin strips	8	8	8
Grated orange zest	15 ml	1 tbsp	1 tbsp
Fresh orange juice	300 ml	½ pt	1¼ cups
Caster (superfine) sugar	45 ml	3 tbsp	3 tbsp

1 Heat the wok or a large heavy-based frying pan.

2 Pour in the oil and when hot stir-fry the pancake strips for about 3–4 minutes.

3 Add all the remaining ingredients, stir well and heat through for a few minutes.

4 Serve hot.

PREPARATION TIME: **COOKING TIME:**
5 MINUTES **7 MINUTES**

Pumpkin Pud

SERVES 4	METRIC	IMPERIAL	AMERICAN
Pumpkin	450 g	1 lb	1 lb
Oil	15 ml	1 tbsp	1 tbsp
Pecan nuts, halved	75 g	3 oz	¾ cup
Ground cinnamon	2.5 ml	½ tsp	½ tsp
Grated nutmeg	2.5 ml	½ tsp	½ tsp
Golden (light corn) syrup	15 ml	1 tbsp	1 tbsp
Brown sugar	15 ml	1 tbsp	1 tbsp
Water	60 ml	4 tbsp	4 tbsp

1 Peel and seed the pumpkin and cut the flesh into 1 cm/½ in cubes.

2 Heat the wok or a large heavy-based frying pan.

3 Pour in the oil and when very hot stir-fry the nuts for about a minute or until they are browned.

4 Add the pumpkin to the pan and stir-fry for 4–5 minutes so that it has softened slightly.

5 Add the remaining ingredients, cover the pan and reduce the heat slightly.

6 Simmer for about 3–4 minutes until the pumpkin is tender but not mushy and then serve hot.

PREPARATION TIME: 10 MINUTES   COOKING TIME: 10 MINUTES

Hot Lemon Delight

SERVES 4	METRIC	IMPERIAL	AMERICAN
Lemon juice	45 ml	3 tbsp	3 tbsp
Plain lemon cake, cubed	225 g	8 oz	8 oz
Oil	30 ml	2 tbsp	2 tbsp
Lemon curd	45 ml	3 tbsp	3 tbsp

1   Pour the lemon juice over the cake and leave to soak for 10 minutes.

2   Heat the wok or a large heavy-based frying pan.

3   Pour in the oil and when hot add the cake and stir-fry for 1–2 minutes so that the cake is slightly browned at the edges.

4   Gently stir in the lemon curd so that the cake does not break up, heat through and serve hot.

PREPARATION TIME:
2 MINUTES PLUS
10 MINUTES
SOAKING TIME

COOKING TIME:
4 MINUTES

Brandy Apples

SERVES 4	METRIC	IMPERIAL	AMERICAN
Oil	*30 ml*	*2 tbsp*	*2 tbsp*
Firm eating (dessert) apples, peeled, cored and sliced	*750 g*	*1½ lb*	*1½ lb*
Brandy	*30 ml*	*2 tbsp*	*2 tbsp*
Icing (confectioners') sugar	*45 ml*	*3 tbsp*	*3 tbsp*

1   Heat the wok or a large heavy-based frying pan.

2   Pour in the oil and when hot add the apples and cook for 3–4 minutes until they are slightly tender and tinged brown.

3   Pour on the brandy and cook for several minutes to evaporate some of the brandy.

4   Dredge with the icing sugar and serve hot.

PREPARATION TIME: COOKING TIME:
10 MINUTES   8 MINUTES

Pears with Cinnamon and Seeds

SERVES 4	METRIC	IMPERIAL	AMERICAN
Oil	15–30 ml	1–2 tbsp	1–2 tbsp
Pumpkin seeds	15 ml	1 tbsp	1 tbsp
Sunflower seeds	15 ml	1 tbsp	1 tbsp
Sesame seeds	15 ml	1 tbsp	1 tbsp
Pears, peeled, cored and thinly sliced	3	3	3
Soft brown sugar	25 ml	1½ tbsp	1½ tbsp
Lemon juice	15 ml	1 tbsp	1 tbsp
Ground cinnamon	15 ml	1 tbsp	1 tbsp

1   Heat the wok or a large heavy-based frying pan.

2   Pour in the oil and when hot add all the seeds and stir-fry until they are crisp but not burnt – this will probably take only a few seconds.

3   Add the pears and cook for another minute.

4   Carefully stir in the sugar, juice and cinnamon being careful not to break the pear slices.

5   Heat through.

SERVING SUGGESTION

Serve with chilled cream or yoghurt.

PREPARATION TIME:
3 MINUTES

COOKING TIME:
4 MINUTES

Sweet Polenta

SERVES 4	METRIC	IMPERIAL	AMERICAN
Water	400 ml	14 fl oz	2 cups
Lemon juice	60 ml	4 tbsp	4 tbsp
Coarse-grain cornmeal	100 g	4 oz	1 cup
Finely grated lemon zest	60 ml	4 tbsp	4 tbsp
Brown sugar	30 ml	2 tbsp	2 tbsp
Honey	60 ml	4 tsp	4 tsp
Ground cinnamon	10 ml	2 tsp	2 tsp
Ground cloves	5 ml	1 tsp	1 tsp
Plain (all-purpose) flour	20 ml	4 tsp	4 tsp
Oil	60 ml	4 tbsp	4 tbsp
Greek-style natural yoghurt	120 ml	4 fl oz	½ cup

1   Bring the water and lemon juice to the boil in a saucepan and shower in the cornmeal.

2   Whisk the mixture constantly until it thickens and starts to leave the sides of the pan.

3   Stir in the lemon zest, sugar and 30 ml/2 tbsp of the honey, then pour the mixture into a shallow container lined with clingfilm (plastic wrap).

4   Place the polenta in the refrigerator for at least 1 hour.

5   Turn the polenta out of the dish and cut into 2.5 cm/1 in cubes.

6   Mix together the cinnamon, cloves and flour and use to coat the cubes.

7   Heat the wok or a large heavy-based frying pan.

8 Pour in the oil and when hot stir-fry the cubes in small batches for 1–2 minutes until slightly browned all over.

9 Lift out the cubes with a draining spoon and divide between two dessert bowls.

10 Top the cubes with the Greek yoghurt, then the remaining honey and eat immediately.

PREPARATION TIME:
5 MINUTES PLUS
15 MINUTES TO MAKE THE
POLENTA AND 1 HOUR
FOR THE POLENTA TO SET

COOKING TIME:
6 MINUTES

Whisky Bread Pudding

SERVES 4	METRIC	IMPERIAL	AMERICAN
Thick white bread slices	4	4	4
Egg, beaten	1	1	1
Whisky	25 ml	1½ tbsp	1½ tbsp
Mixed (apple-pie) spice	10 ml	2 tsp	2 tsp
Single (light) cream	65 ml	4½ tbsp	4½ tbsp
Oil	30 ml	2 tbsp	2 tbsp
Demerara sugar	30 ml	2 tbsp	2 tbsp
Sultanas (golden raisins)	30 ml	2 tbsp	2 tbsp
Raisins	15 ml	1 tbsp	1 tbsp

1   Remove and discard the crusts and cut the bread into 2.5 cm/ 1 in cubes.

2   Combine the beaten egg, whisky, mixed spice and 25 ml/ 1½ tbsp of the cream and pour over the bread cubes. Mix well and leave to soak for 10 minutes.

3   Heat the wok or a large heavy-based frying pan.

4   Pour in the oil and when hot stir-fry the soaked bread cubes for 1–2 minutes until they are browned on all sides.

5   Drain off any excess oil, then quickly stir in the remaining cream, the sugar and dried fruit.

6   Heat through for a few seconds, then serve hot.

PREPARATION TIME:
5 MINUTES PLUS 10
MINUTES TO SOAK
THE BREAD

COOKING TIME:
3 MINUTES

INDEX